Culinary Arts Institute

The Complete Book of Creative
CREPES

Featured in cover photo:
Coral Shrimp, 47

The Complete Book of Creative

THE COMPLETE BOOK OF CREATIVE CREPES

Barbara Prinzivalli, Carol Statemen, and
the Culinary Arts Institute Staff:

Helen Geist: Director
Sherrill Corley: Editor • Helen Lehman: Assistant Editor
Edward Finnegan: Executive Editor • Charles Bozett: Art Director
Ethel La Roche: Editorial Assistant • Ivanka Simatic: Recipe Tester
Malinda Miller: Copy Editor • John Mahalek: Art Assembly

Book designed and coordinated by Charles Bozett and Laurel DiGangi

Illustrations by Justin Wager

Photographs by Zdenek Pivecka

CREPES

Culinary Arts Institute

1727 South Indiana Avenue, Chicago, Illinois 60616

INTRODUCTION

Crepe is French for a delicate thin pancake which can be served as a tempting part of breakfast, an interesting appetizer, a tasty entrée, or a delicious dessert. Crepes can be sweetened for desserts, toasted or dipped for snacks, and served plain or flavored for main courses.

Cooking with crepes isn't new. Every nationality has its variation of the crepe—the Russian blini with caviar, the Jewish blintz with fruit and sour cream, the Mexican tortilla with frijoles, the Scandinavian fyllda pannkakor, the Hungarian walnut palacsinta. Italians have manicotti, and the egg roll belongs to the Orient. These are just a few examples of the versatility of this delicate pancake.

Why are crepes so popular? Maybe it's because a crepe dessert can be as easy as a few drops of lemon juice and powdered sugar or as elegant as flaming crepes suzette. Perhaps it's because you can make an appetizer or dinner for company with leftover meats and a sauce. Or stretch a pound of seafood to feed the whole family. You can be the perfect hostess and enjoy the party by keeping a variety of crepe fillings stored in the refrigerator ready to make four or five different types of hors d'oeuvres for a crowd in less than half an hour. The fact that crepes store easily in the refrigerator or freezer and that you can serve them after a minimal amount of time in the kitchen in an unending list of ways is why so many people have made crepes a popular part of their eating pleasures.

In this book, CULINARY ARTS INSTITUTE has tried to give you a complete look at the versatility of the crepe. Included are numerous recipes for delicious dining and entertaining, as well as ways to create your own culinary masterpieces. You can let your creative imagination rule and use crepes where you previously used rice, noodles, crackers, biscuits, and bread.

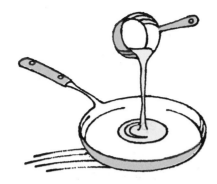

CONTENTS

ABOUT CREPES

CREPE PANS

Success in making crepes starts with the selection of the pan. There are many pans on the market, but some are better suited for crepes than others. Here's what to look for:

—Light weight
—Shallow design with slanting sides
—Bottom diameter of about six inches
—Handle equal in length to pan width for easy swirling
—Even-heating metal

When it comes to the choice of metal, you have some latitude. Some rave about cast aluminum, while others claim that a black steel pan is the only one to use.

Some prefer to cook crepes the traditional way (inside the pan) using either a regular 6- to 8-inch skillet or a pan designed for making crepes. Some traditional pan designs are illustrated below.

And still others prefer to cook the crepe *on* the pan, bottom-side up, rather than *in* the pan. Such dome-shaped pans usually come with step-by-step instructions, and operate on the principle sometimes used in crepe restaurants: the pan is heated upside down, then the bottom is dipped in batter, and the pan is returned to the heat, upside down, to cook the crepe. Using this method, you cook the crepe on one side only, without turning. Some "upside-down" pans are illustrated below.

Electric crepe pans are available in both traditional and "upside-down" pans. These pans are usually more expensive than nonelectric ones, but they do maintain a constant temperature during cooking. Pans with nonstick finishes are also available. When using these pans, little or no fat is required to prevent the crepes from sticking, the crepes are relatively easy to turn or flip, and the pan is easy to clean without removing the seasoning.

Check the manufacturer's directions that come with your pan to see if there are any specific instructions—or prohibitions—about seasoning. If there are none, wash the pan, then grease the cooking surface with vegetable oil or shortening. Place the pan over very low heat and, as the grease melts, wipe off the excess with a paper towel. Continue heating for 5 to 15 minutes, depending upon the weight of your pan. The pan should just be warm to the touch. Then remove it from the heat and let stand overnight before using.

To keep your pan well seasoned, don't wash it after crepe-making. Instead, just wipe it clean with an oiled paper towel.

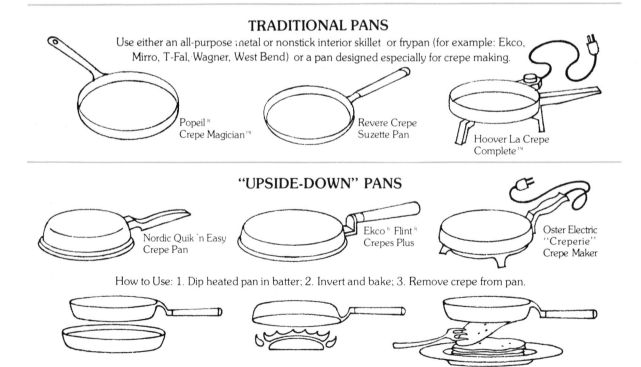

TRADITIONAL PANS

Use either an all-purpose metal or nonstick interior skillet or frypan (for example: Ekco, Mirro, T-Fal, Wagner, West Bend) or a pan designed especially for crepe making.

Popeil ® Crepe Magician ™

Revere Crepe Suzette Pan

Hoover La Crepe Complete ™

"UPSIDE-DOWN" PANS

Nordic Quik 'n Easy Crepe Pan

Ekco ® Flint ® Crepes Plus

Oster Electric "Creperie" Crepe Maker

How to Use: 1. Dip heated pan in batter; 2. Invert and bake; 3. Remove crepe from pan.

BASIC CREPES

Dinner Crepes

1 cup all-purpose flour
⅛ teaspoon salt
3 eggs
1½ cups milk
2 tablespoons melted butter or oil

1. Sift flour and salt. Add eggs, one at a time, beating thoroughly. Gradually add milk, mixing until blended. Add melted butter or oil and beat until smooth. (Or mix in an electric blender until smooth.)
2. Let batter stand for 1 hour before cooking crepes.

About 18 crepes

Dessert Crepes

1 cup all-purpose flour
¼ cup sugar
   Pinch salt
3 eggs
1½ cups milk
2 tablespoons melted butter or oil
2 tablespoons brandy

1. Sift flour, sugar, and salt. Add eggs, one at a time, beating thoroughly. Gradually add milk, melted butter or oil, and brandy, beating until smooth. (Or mix in an electric blender until smooth.)
2. Let batter stand 1 hour before cooking crepes.

About 18 crepes

Cocoa Crepes: Follow recipe for Dessert Crepes; then mix **2 tablespoons cocoa** with flour, sugar, and salt, and substitute **2 tablespoons rum** for brandy.

THE TRADITIONAL WAY TO COOK A CREPE

Heat a 6-inch crepe pan. Brush with oil. When oil is hot, remove pan from heat, pour in 3 tablespoons of batter. Swirl pan quickly to cover bottom of pan; if there are holes, fill in the holes with more batter. Return to heat. Cook until golden brown, turn crepe over, and cook reverse side (about ½ minute on each side). Turn crepe out on a piece of waxed paper or toweling. The cooked crepes can be stacked on a plate and kept warm in a low oven, and used immediately. Or, after they have cooled, they can be stacked, covered, and stored in refrigerator; or stacked, wrapped in foil or freezer bags, and frozen. Bring to room temperature before trying to separate.

HOW TO MAKE YOUR OWN CREPE RECIPE

We have included our basic crepe recipes, but you can create your own. The basic proportions that we use are 1 egg, ⅓ cup flour, and ½ cup milk. You can vary the flour up to ½ cup or increase the milk to make a thinner batter. When increasing the liquid, if it is hard to handle, use cream as part of the liquid. You can also substitute pancake mix for flour in the basic recipe, use only 2 eggs, and increase milk to 1½ cups. You can add your own creative touches to the basic recipe.

For Dinner Crepes add or substitute:
—1 tablespoon brandy or sherry
—Beer, bouillon, or juice for part of the milk
—Minced fresh (2 teaspoons) or dried (¾ teaspoon) herbs
—¾ teaspoon grated lemon, lime, or tangerine peel
—Dash of cayenne pepper or Tabasco
—½ teaspoon curry powder
—Mashed vegetables for part of flour
—For low carbohydrate crepes, decrease flour, increase eggs, and substitute heavy cream and water for milk.
—For low calorie crepes, substitute broth for milk and decrease oil to 1 tablespoon.

For Dessert Crepes add or substitute:
—½ teaspoon vanilla, almond, or fruit extract
—½ teaspoon maple, chocolate, or peppermint flavoring
—1 to 2 tablespoons Grand Marnier, curaçao, Cointreau, crème de cacao, or Kaluha
—1 tablespoon finely chopped nuts
—Sour cream for some of the milk
—A pinch of cinnamon
—Mashed cooked fruit for some of flour
—Finely crushed macaroons for some of the flour
—Fruit juice for part of the milk

In the following two recipes, we have substituted different types of flour. Both batters tend to separate; stir occasionally to keep blended.

Wheat Crepes

1 cup whole wheat flour
1 tablespoon sprouted wheat or wheat germ
3 eggs
Pinch salt
½ cup whipping cream
¾ cup water
2 tablespoons butter or margarine, melted

Make batter the same way as basic crepes (page 11).
About 16 crepes

Corn Crepes

⅔ cup all-purpose flour
6 tablespoons cornmeal
3 eggs
Pinch salt
1 cup milk or cream
2 tablespoons oil

Make batter the same way as basic crepes (page 11).
About 10 crepes

WHAT TO DO WITH BROKEN CREPES
Dinner Crepes
1. Cut into strips and use as noodles in soup.
2. Cut into strips and bake at 375°F 10 minutes; use as a substitute for fried Chinese noodles.

Dessert Crepes
1. Cut in strips, dip in sweetened condensed milk, and toss with chopped nuts and flaked coconut. Bake at 375°F 10 minutes.
2. Cut in strips and roll around miniature marshmallows or small pieces of fruit. Spear with wooden pick. Dip in melted chocolate. Put on waxed paper and refrigerate 1 hour.

WHAT TO DO IF YOUR CREPE IS:
Too thick: Beat 1 to 2 tablespoons more milk into batter.
Too rubbery: Decrease amount of eggs.
Too thin: Increase flour or let batter rest longer before using.
Too delicate: Decrease liqueur, if used, or increase eggs.
Too brown: Decrease sugar.
Too pale: Add a little more sugar.

METHODS OF ASSEMBLY

JELLY-ROLL METHOD: Spread crepe with filling according to recipe. Lift edge and fold under. Roll up firmly.

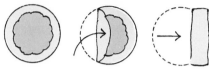

EGG-ROLL METHOD: Place filling in a line down the center of the crepe, leaving enough space at either end of the filling to fold crepe up and over the filling. Lift edge and tuck around and under filling. Roll up firmly.

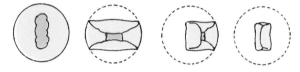

TUBE METHOD: Place filling in a line down the center of the crepe. Lift edge and tuck under filling. Roll up firmly.

HOT SAUCE METHOD: This method is usually done in a chafing dish or electric fry pan (set at 325°F) in which a sauce is heated.

Each crepe is coated with the sauce on both sides by placing a crepe in the heated sauce, turning it over (using two spoons or two forks), folding in half and then in half again. Push to one side. Continue until all crepes are coated.

TURNOVER METHOD: Using a slotted spoon, place filling on one half of the crepe, leaving a ¼- to ½-inch border. Moisten the back of a spoon with sauce from the filling. Run moistened spoon along rim of crepe. Fold crepe in half and press along rim to seal.

SQUARE TURNOVER METHOD: Spoon about 2 to 3 tablespoons of filling into center of crepe. Fold two opposite sides into center so they overlap. Fold the other two sides into the center to make a square package with all filling enclosed.

TART METHOD: This method makes a pretty tart with a fluted edge. Each crepe is put into a well in a muffin pan, an individual ramekin, or custard dish. It is then given a filling and baked to set filling.

To form the tart, center the crepe over the muffin well and fit it in, folding the edges slightly until it forms a cup. The muffin pan will become overcrowded if each well is used, so stagger the crepes in the pan so that they fit comfortably.

Fill the crepe tart with one mixture or alternate mixtures, a tablespoon at a time. Ease crepe and filling all the way down into the muffin cup. Spoon a topping over filling and bake. Be careful not to spill any filling or topping into the muffin cup. Each tart holds up to 3 to 4 tablespoons of filling. Do not overfill. The tart should have a fluted or ruffled look.

Most tarts are baked in two stages to insure they are cooked through and filling is solid. Cool 10, 15, or 20 minutes before removing from cup. These can be served on a plate as you would a pastry tart.

BUTTERFLY METHOD: In this method, the crepes are assembled on an individual serving plate. You will use 1½ crepes, a filling, a topping, and garnishes to create the appearance of a butterfly. The effect is created by placing the filling in 2 parallel rows on the whole crepe (A). Using the half-crepe, fold into a "V" (B). Place fold between rows of filling. Gently release crepe, draping it over filling (C). Spoon or pipe topping down center fold. Garnishes on top crepe half are patterned to give the appearance of butterfly wings. Garnish for antennas according to recipe (D).

A WORD ABOUT FILLINGS

Fillings can be any flavor as long as they are thick but spreadable and not too moist. Usually 1½ to 2 tablespoons of a spread will cover one crepe.

Tarts: The fillings can be moist when assembled but should be firm when baked—a cooked, drained meat topped with a thick cheese mixture is easy to work with. Fresh fruits which weep when baked, raw meat which renders juice and fat, jelly which saturates and sticks when baked are not good fillings because the bottom of the tart stays wet and can't be removed from the cup. Be careful not to spill any filling or topping between the crepe and the cup—it will cause it to stick.

Tubes, turnovers, and egg rolls: Fillings for these are the most versatile. They can be chopped meats, diced vegetables, sliced fruit, or seafood, with or without a sauce inside and/or on top.

Stacks: The filling for these should be thick if it is spreadable, drained if it is in a sauce or has juice, or a crumb mixture that can be broiled. The ease of slicing and serving a stack depends on the filling. If it is too soft or wet the stacks tend to slide apart. You can blend flavors by putting different fillings on different layers—a crepe, chicken spread; a crepe, mushroom spread; a crepe, drained cooked spinach. Then bake and serve with a sauce.

STORAGE HINTS

BATTER: Store in a small, covered container for 1 to 2 days. It may need to be thinned with more milk before using.

FILLING: Most fillings store well in a covered container in the refrigerator for 2 to 3 days. Some can be frozen, and this is usually noted in the recipe.

CREPES: Crepes that are cooked on both sides store easily stacked in piles of 4, 8, or 12, wrapped in foil and refrigerated or frozen. To store crepes that are cooked only on one side (dome pans), separate each one with waxed paper, wrap, and refrigerate or freeze. It takes only a few minutes for them to defrost.

FILLED CREPES: Filled crepes can be wrapped in plastic and refrigerated for 2 to 3 days, or frozen for 1 week to a month. To reheat, bring up to room temperature and bake according to recipe. If the recipe calls for a sauce, freeze it separately or make it up fresh.

HORS D'OEUVRES AND SPREADS

Wafer Crepes

2½ cups crepe batter (see Note)
Cooking oil

1. Heat a skillet or griddle over medium heat, and brush with oil.
2. Pour ½ tablespoon batter in skillet, but do not swirl the pan. Pour 3 or 4 more crepes, turn when brown, and brown on other side. Place crepes on ungreased baking sheet.
3. Bake at 350°F about 15 minutes, turning over halfway through baking. Remove from baking sheet and serve with dips, spreads, or cheese.

About 8 dozen wafers

Note: Any of the crepe batters may be used to make Wafer Crepes. If desired, batter may be thinned with a little liquid for thinner, crisper wafers.

Pinwheel Party Platter
(with Turkey, Ham, and Asparagus)

½ pound mushrooms, cleaned and chopped
5 tablespoons butter or margarine
5 tablespoons flour
½ cup water
½ cup whipping cream
¼ teaspoon salt
2 dashes pepper
¼ teaspoon dry mustard
Dash cayenne pepper
¼ pound Swiss cheese, shredded
15 dinner crepes
10 asparagus spears, cooked and salted
5 (1-ounce) slices boiled ham
5 (1-ounce) slices cooked turkey breast, lightly salted

1. Lightly sauté mushrooms in 1 tablespoon butter about 3 minutes. Set aside.
2. Melt remaining butter over low heat. Add flour and stir until smooth. Slowly stir in water and cream. Add mushrooms. Over medium heat, stir and bring to boiling. Blend in dry seasonings and Swiss cheese. Cook and stir until cheese melts.
3. Spread mixture over crepes. Pinwheels are made by placing a ham or turkey slice, tightly rolled around one asparagus spear, at the bottom edge of each crepe. Roll up, forming a tight roll. Put into a baking dish.
4. Bake at 375°F 10 minutes. Cool 30 minutes.
5. Slice each roll into 6 pinwheels. Serve with picks. Arrange in a colorful pattern on a platter.

90 hors d'oeuvres

Dilled Beef Rolls

⅓ cup dairy sour cream
2 tablespoons grated cucumber
⅛ teaspoon dill weed
Dash Worcestershire sauce
1 can (4½ ounces) roast beef spread
4 dinner crepes

1. Combine sour cream, cucumber, dill weed, and Worcestershire sauce. Let stand 30 minutes.
2. Spread roast beef mixture on the crepes. Top with a thin layer of sour cream mixture. Roll up jelly-roll fashion. Place on a cookie sheet.
3. Bake at 375°F 15 minutes.
4. Cut each roll into thirds and serve warm as a snack or hors d'oeuvres.

1 dozen hors d'oeuvres

Ingredients for Dinner Crepes, 11

Anchovy Bits

4 dinner crepes
½ cup shredded mozzarella
  cheese
8 to 16 anchovy fillets packed in
  oil, drained
¼ teaspoon garlic powder
½ teaspoon oregano

1. On each crepe sprinkle mozzarella cheese, top with 2 to 4 (depending on taste) anchovy fillets, and sprinkle with garlic powder and oregano.
2. Roll up jelly-roll fashion. Place on a cookie sheet.
3. Bake at 375°F 10 minutes.
4. Rolls can be served individually as appetizers, or each roll can be cut into bite-size pieces and served as hors d'oeuvres.

4 large appetizers or *2 dozen hors d'oeuvres*

Chili Pinwheels

1 can (about 15½ ounces) kidney
  beans
½ teaspoon chili powder
½ pound ground beef
⅓ cup chopped onion
¼ cup chopped green pepper
2 tablespoons ketchup
2 dashes Tabasco
  Salt and pepper
8 dinner crepes or 8 corn crepes
  (see page 12)

1. Drain and mash beans. Blend in chili powder. Set aside.
2. Sauté beef with onion and green pepper. When onion and green pepper are tender, remove from heat and drain off any liquid. Stir ketchup, Tabasco, and bean mixture into drained meat. Season with salt and pepper to taste.
3. For bite-size snacks or hors d'oeuvres, assemble by jelly-roll method.
4. Bake at 375°F 15 minutes. Cool 5 minutes and slice.

8 rolls

Chili Turnovers: Follow recipe for Chili Pinwheels for filling. Assemble by turnover method. Bake at 375°F 15 minutes; serve hot. These can be picked up and eaten like a sandwich.

Sardine Pinwheels

1 can (1½ ounces) sardines in oil
1 scallion, minced
½ teaspoon dry mustard
1 to 2 tablespoons dairy sour cream
  Salt and pepper
6 dinner crepes

1. Drain and mash sardines; stir in scallion, mustard, and just enough sour cream to make it spreadable. Season to taste with salt and pepper.
2. Spread on crepes and roll up jelly-roll fashion. Slice into bite-size pieces (about 6 per crepe).

About 3 dozen hors d'oeuvres

Red Reuben

1 can (4½ ounces) corned beef
  spread
4 dinner crepes
½ cup drained canned sweet 'n' sour
  red cabbage
½ cup shredded Swiss cheese

1. Smooth ¼ can of corned beef spread on each crepe: spread 2 tablespoons of red cabbage over corned beef. Sprinkle with 2 tablespoons cheese.
2. Roll up jelly-roll fashion.
3. Bake at 375°F 10 minutes.
4. Serve one or two as a snack or slice into bite-size pieces for hors d'oeuvres. If desired, spear with picks and dip into Dijon Sauce (see page 84).

4 rolls or *2 dozen hors d'oeuvres*

Nippy Beef Spread with Wafer Crepes, 16
(Tray from outer edge to center): Fried Cheese Rolls, 18;
Chili-Nut Log, 19; Chili Pinwheels, 17; Cocktail Frank
Wrap-Ups, 20

Herring and Beets

4 ounces drained canned beets, minced
1 jar (5 ounces) pickled herring, drained and cut in bite-size pieces
¼ cup dairy sour cream
6 dinner crepes

1. Combine beets, herring pieces, and sour cream. Let stand at least 1 hour.
2. Assemble, using square turnover method; drain filling with a slotted spoon.
3. Serve topped with remaining sour cream sauce.

6 servings

Cheese Roll-Ups

Filling:
1 cup creamed cottage cheese
1 tablespoon lemon juice
¼ teaspoon seasoned salt
16 dinner crepes or 16 wheat crepes (see page 12)

Toppings:
1 tablespoon chopped lox or smoked salmon
1 tablespoon sautéed onion with a pinch of curry powder
1 teaspoon grated cucumber and 1 teaspoon grated carrot
1 tablespoon chopped pimento-stuffed olives
2 teaspoons minced Bermuda onion
2 teaspoons bacon bits and 1 teaspoon grated Parmesan cheese
2 teaspoons chopped scallions
2 teaspoons grated cucumber and 1 tablespoon chopped tomato
⅛ teaspoon dill weed
2 teaspoons caviar

1. Combine cheese, lemon juice, and salt in an electric blender. Blend on medium speed until smooth. Chill 1 hour.
2. To assemble, spread crepe with a rounded tablespoon of cottage cheese mixture. Top with any one of the toppings listed.
3. Cut each crepe into 6 wedges. Roll up each wedge starting with wide end. Serve with picks.

8 dozen hors d'oeuvres

Fried Cheese Roll

6 (1-ounce) wedges Gruyère cheese
6 dinner crepes
2 eggs, beaten
⅓ cup fine dry bread crumbs, seasoned or plain
Oil for frying heated to 375°F

1. Coarsely shred 1 wedge of cheese over 1 crepe to within 1 inch of crepe edges. Fold two opposite sides of crepe over 1 inch. Continue folding as directed in egg-roll method. Dip rolls into eggs. Coat thoroughly with bread crumbs.
2. Fry in 375°F oil until golden brown (about 5 minutes). Cool slightly. Cut into 1-inch pieces and serve.

6 cheese rolls

Cheddar-Nut Log

8 ounces sharp Cheddar cheese
  spread
¼ cup chopped nuts
1 tablespoon chopped parsley
3 dinner crepes
  Paprika

1. Blend cheese, nuts, and parsley well. Refrigerate 30 minutes.
2. Form mixture into 3 logs. Place a log on one end of each crepe and roll. Sprinkle log with paprika. Freeze 1 hour.
3. Slice while frozen. Spear with picks and serve at room temperature.

3 nut logs

Herbed Cheese Log

1 package (8 ounces) cream
  cheese
1 medium clove garlic, crushed in
  a garlic press
1 teaspoon grated onion
⅓ cup chopped fresh parsley
3 dinner crepes

1. Blend cheese, garlic, onion, and 1 tablespoon parsley. Refrigerate 30 minutes.
2. Form mixture into 3 logs. Place a log on one end of each crepe and roll. Roll log in remaining parsley. Freeze 1 hour.
3. Slice roll while frozen. Spear with picks. Serve when cheese is at room temperature.

3 cheese logs

Note: If desired, substitute an herbed cheese such as Boursin for the cheese mixture.

Chili-Nut Log

8 ounces process sharp Cheddar
  cheese spread (at room
  temperature)
2 tablespoons butter or margarine
  (at room temperature)
½ teaspoon minced onion
¼ teaspoon minced garlic
1 tablespoon chili powder
  Dash cayenne pepper
2 tablespoons lemon juice
⅓ cup finely chopped walnuts or
  pecans
3 dinner crepes
  Melted butter or margarine
2 tablespoons chopped parsley

1. Combine cheese, 2 tablespoons butter, onion, garlic, chili powder, cayenne, lemon juice, and nuts. Mix until well blended. Shape into 3 or 4 logs. (If mixture is too soft to work with, refrigerate for 10 to 15 minutes.)
2. Place log at one end of crepe and roll up. Brush outside of crepe with melted butter and roll in parsley. Refrigerate 10 minutes, slice, and serve with picks.
3. Store in refrigerator up to 1 week, or store in freezer.

3 logs

Cocktail Frank Wrap-Ups

2 dinner crepes
1 teaspoon prepared mustard
1 package (5½ ounces) cocktail frankfurters

1. Spread each crepe on one side with ½ teaspoon mustard. Cut each crepe in 8 wedges. Starting from wide edge, roll up a frankfurter in each wedge. Place seam side down in a shallow baking pan.
2. Bake at 375°F 10 minutes. Spear with wooden picks and serve with **bottled cocktail sauce.**

16 appetizers

Peanut Butter-Banana Roll

¼ cup peanut butter
1 large ripe banana, mashed
4 dessert or dinner crepes

1. Combine peanut butter and banana until well blended.
2. Spread mixture on crepes. Roll up jelly-roll fashion. Slice in half. Serve as a snack.

8 pieces

Seafood Horns

¾ cup chopped cooked seafood (crab-meat, lobster, or shrimp)
¼ cup chopped ripe olives
3 tablespoons mayonnaise
¼ teaspoon lemon juice
Salt and pepper to taste
6 dinner crepes or 6 wheat crepes (see page 12)

1. Combine seafood, olives, mayonnaise, lemon juice, salt, and pepper. Spread about 2½ tablespoons of the mixture on each crepe.
2. Using a sharp knife, slice each crepe into 8 wedges. Roll up each wedge, starting with the wide side and rolling to the tip. Secure with wooden picks. Arrange on a lightly greased baking sheet.
3. Broil, with tops 3 to 4 inches from heat, 1 to 2 minutes.

4 dozen appetizers

Bacon-Nut Log

¼ cup peanut butter
1 tablespoon butter or margarine
4 strips bacon
4 dinner or dessert crepes

1. Blend peanut butter and butter until it spreads more like butter than peanut butter.
2. Fry bacon until crisp; drain and crumble.
3. Spread peanut butter-butter mixture on crepes, sprinkle on bacon pieces, and roll up jelly-roll fashion.
4. Cut each log into 4 pieces. Serve as a snack.

16 pieces

Three-Cheese Nut Roll

1 package (8 ounces) cream cheese (at room temperature)
4 ounces blue cheese
4 ounces sharp Cheddar cheese spread
½ small onion, grated
1 teaspoon Worcestershire sauce
¼ cup chopped nuts
¼ cup chopped parsley
6 dinner crepes
2 tablespoons butter or margarine, melted

1. Combine cheeses, onion, and Worcestershire sauce.
2. Mix nuts and parsley. Blend half of the nut mixture into the cheese mixture. Form into 6 logs.
3. Place a log to one side of each crepe and roll up. Roll in remaining nut-parsley mixture. Freeze 1 hour.
4. Slice, while frozen, into ¼-inch pieces. Serve at room temperature with picks. (No crackers needed!)

6 nut rolls

SPREADS

Crepes lend themselves nicely to being lightly covered with a spread, rolled up, sliced in bite-size pieces, and served. The spread recipes that follow have many things in common. They are easier to spread at room temperature; a thin coating, about ⅛ inch, is all that is necessary. They can be made up in advance; most spreads refrigerate and/or freeze well for convenience. Many are used in other recipes instead of a sauce. There is no need for crackers when you have crepes and a spread.

Mushroom-Garlic Spread

1 pound mushrooms, cleaned and finely chopped
2 tablespoons butter or margarine
1 clove garlic, crushed in a garlic press (or ½ teaspoon garlic powder)
½ teaspoon salt
3 tablespoons finely chopped fresh parsley (or 1½ tablespoons dried parsley)
1 package (8 ounces) cream cheese, softened
Dinner crepes

1. Sauté mushrooms in butter until dark brown. Stir in garlic, salt, and parsley. Simmer 2 minutes. Gradually add cream cheese, stirring until well blended.
2. Spread ⅛ inch thick on each crepe. Roll up jelly-roll fashion. Put into a baking dish.
3. Bake at 375°F 15 minutes. Cut into bite-size pieces and serve.

2 cups spread

Note: Spread can be stored in a covered container in refrigerator for 2 weeks, or it can be frozen.

Shrimp Spread

½ cup butter or margarine, softened
¼ cup lemon juice
3 tablespoons sherry
½ teaspoon dried tarragon
1 teaspoon Dijon mustard
½ teaspoon mace
¼ medium onion
¼ teaspoon pepper
¼ teaspoon salt
¼ teaspoon Tabasco
1 pound frozen shrimp, cooked

Combine all ingredients except shrimp in an electric blender. Blend until smooth. Gradually add shrimp, continuing to blend until smooth.

1 cup spread

Nippy Beef Spread

1 package (3 ounces) vacuum-
  packed wafer-sliced beef,
  finely chopped
1 package (8 ounces) cream cheese
  (at room temperature)
2 tablespoons prepared
  horseradish
1 teaspoon Worcestershire sauce
  Dinner crepes

1. Combine ingredients for spread.
2. Spread a thin layer of mixture over each crepe. Roll up jelly-roll fashion. Chill 30 minutes.
3. Slice into 1-inch pieces and serve.

1½ cups spread

Note: Spread can be stored in a covered container in the refrigerator for 1 week, or it can be frozen.

Lima Bean Spread

1 can (8 ounces) lima beans
1 package (3 ounces) cream cheese
  (at room temperature)
¼ cup dairy sour cream
1 tablespoon very finely
  chopped onion
½ teaspoon lemon juice
2 drops Tabasco
¼ teaspoon seasoned salt
⅛ teaspoon Worcestershire sauce
  Dash cayenne pepper
1 tablespoon bacon pieces or
  minced ham

Drain beans; mash. Add cream cheese and blend well. Stir in sour cream, onion, lemon juice, Tabasco, salt, Worcestershire sauce, cayenne, and bacon or ham.

About 1 cup spread

Note: The spread stores well, tightly covered in refrigerator.

Braunschweiger-Burgundy Spread

½ pound Braunschweiger (at room
  temperature)
1 small onion, grated
½ medium green pepper, finely
  chopped
3 drops Tabasco
  Burgundy

Combine Braunschweiger, onion, green pepper, and Tabasco. Gradually add burgundy, mashing until mixture is spreadable.

1 cup spread

Olive-Cheese Spread

4 ounces process sharp Cheddar
   cheese spread (at room
   temperature)
1 tablespoon butter or
   margarine (at room
   temperature)
   Dash cayenne pepper
1 teaspoon chili sauce
¼ cup chopped ripe olives

1. Combine all ingredients; mix until well blended.
2. Spread a thin layer of spread on each crepe. Roll up jelly-roll fashion; slice into bite-size pieces. Serve with picks.

⅔ cup spread

Note: Spread can be stored in a covered container in the refrigerator for 1 week, or it can be frozen.

Sherried Chicken Liver Spread

1 large onion, coarsely
   chopped
¼ cup rendered chicken fat
½ pound chicken livers
¼ teaspoon thyme
1 tablespoon sherry
   Salt and pepper

1. Sauté onion in chicken fat 5 minutes. Add chicken livers, thyme, and sherry. Cook 5 minutes longer, or until livers are cooked through.
2. Chop mixture finely or put through a food grinder. Add salt and pepper to taste; mix well. Consistency should be that of a thick paste; thin with sherry if necessary.

1 cup spread

DIP A CREPE

Beef in Horseradish

   Chopped meat
1 package (8 ounces) cream cheese,
   softened
1 tablespoon prepared
   horseradish
1 can (about 10 ounces)
   condensed cream of mushroom
   soup
   Dinner crepes

1. Make logs from meat. Pan-fry them until browned on all sides.
2. Beat cream cheese, horseradish, and condensed soup together until smooth.
3. Spread a thin layer of sauce on crepe; place meat log on crepe and roll up jelly-roll fashion. Slice in quarters; spear with picks. Accompany with remaining sauce.

Vegetables in Béarnaise

Cooked broccoli, asparagus,
 or cauliflower
Dinner crepes
Béarnaise Sauce (see page
 84)

Wrap vegetable pieces in crepes, jelly-roll fashion. Slice, spear with picks, and serve with sauce.

Variation: Substitute **Russian dressing** for Béarnaise Sauce.

Sausages in Cream

Dinner crepes
Salad mustard
Italian sausages
1 cup dairy sour cream
1 tablespoon Dijon mustard
Dash Worcestershire sauce

1. Spread crepe with salad mustard. Put 1 sausage on crepe and roll up jelly-roll fashion. Slice into quarters; spear with picks.
2. Combine sour cream, Dijon mustard, and Worcestershire sauce for dipping sauce.

Fruit in Chocolate

Banana strips or pineapple
 spears
Dessert crepes
Hot fudge sauce*

Wrap fruit in crepe. Slice, spear with picks, and serve with sauce.

*Or use a sauce of **1 large chocolate bar,** melted, and desired amount of **coffee liqueur.**

Variation: Substitute **fruited yogurt** for hot fudge sauce.

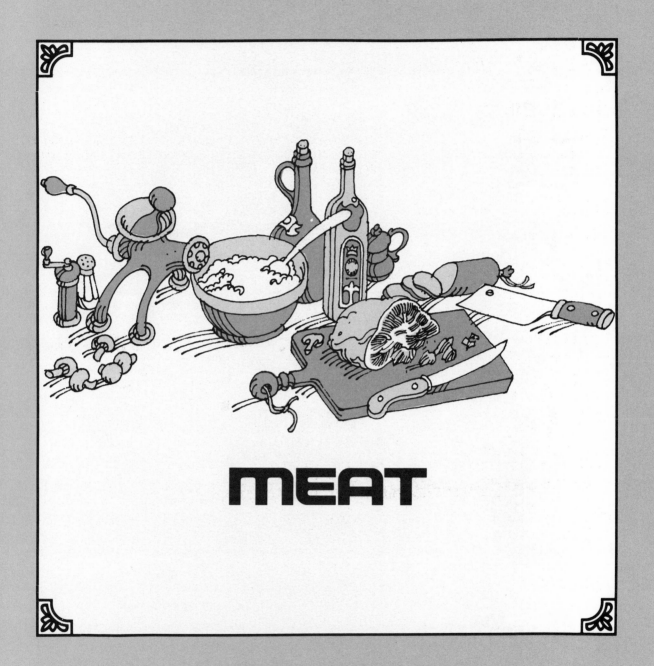

MEAT

Beef Stroganoff Turnovers

2 tablespoons butter or
   margarine
½ medium onion, minced
½ pound mushrooms, cleaned and
   sliced
1 pound skirt steak, cut in
   thin strips (sirloin,
   round, or flank can be
   substituted)
1 medium clove garlic, crushed in a
   garlic press
⅛ teaspoon cumin
⅛ teaspoon dill weed
⅛ teaspoon marjoram
1 teaspoon Worcestershire sauce
2 tablespoons ketchup
⅓ cup red wine
1 beef bouillon cube
   Salt and pepper
8 ounces dairy sour cream
6 dinner crepes

1. Melt butter. Sauté onion and mushrooms. Add meat strips, garlic, cumin, dill weed, marjoram, Worcestershire sauce, and ketchup. Sauté until meat is browned. Stir in wine and bouillon cube. Simmer until meat is tender. Season with salt and pepper to taste. Stir in sour cream. Cook over low heat 5 minutes.
2. Using a slotted spoon, assemble by turnover method. Place on baking sheet.
3. Bake at 350°F 10 minutes. Serve topped with any remaining sauce.

6 turnovers

Steak and Kidney Pie

½ pound lamb kidneys
⅓ cup butter or margarine
1 cup chopped onion
½ pound diced beef (top sirloin,
   round, or flank)
1 cup dry red wine
¼ teaspoon marjoram
1 small clove garlic, crushed in
   a garlic press
1 tablespoon flour
¾ cup beef broth (1 beef
   bouillon cube dissolved in ¾ cup
   boiling water)
   Salt and pepper
6 dinner crepes

1. Peel, core, and dice kidneys.
2. Melt butter. Sauté kidneys over low heat until browned. Add onion and beef. Continue cooking until onion is browned and meat is tender. Stir in wine, marjoram, and garlic. Simmer, covered, 15 minutes.
3. Stir in flour. Gradually add broth, stirring constantly. Cook until sauce thickens. Add salt and pepper to taste.
4. Assemble, using tube method. Arrange, seam side down, on a baking sheet.
5. Bake at 375°F 10 minutes. Crepe will be crisp but filling will be moist and tasty. Serve immediately.

6 filled crepes

Note: One crepe, accompanied by soup, salad, vegetable, and dessert, is a filling dinner.

Italian Meat Rolls

1 pound chopped beef
½ cup coarsely shredded
   mozzarella cheese
½ cup grated Parmesan cheese
1 tablespoon chopped fresh
   parsley
4 eggs

1. Combine meat, cheeses, parsley, 2 eggs, and garlic powder.
2. Remove tomatoes from liquid and coarsely chop. Press in strainer to remove remaining liquid. Blend tomato pulp into meat. Carefully fold in peas. Divide into 6 loaves approximately 5 inches long. Put into a baking dish.
3. Bake the logs at 350°F 20 minutes. Cool 10 minutes.

¼ teaspoon garlic powder
1 can (16 ounces) tomatoes
1 can (16 ounces) green peas
6 dinner crepes
  Bread crumbs
  Oil for deep frying heated to
    375°F

4. Assemble by egg-roll method, using meat logs for filling.
5. Beat 2 eggs. Dip filled rolls into eggs. Roll lightly in bread crumbs.
6. Fry in heated deep fat 5 minutes, or until golden brown.
7. Serve meat rolls hot. If desired, top with Italian tomato sauce and grated Parmesan cheese.

6 filled crepes

Note: Meat rolls can be stored in the refrigerator or freezer. To reheat, bring the rolls to room temperature. Bake at 375°F 10 to 12 minutes.

Beef and Mushroom Wellington

3 tablespoons oil
3 tablespoons lemon juice
1 medium clove garlic, crushed in a garlic press
1 flank steak (about 1¼ pounds)
  Salt and pepper
2 cups Mushroom-Garlic Spread (see page 21)
12 dinner crepes
2 cups Mushroom Sauce (see page 88)

1. To prepare marinade, mix oil, lemon juice, and garlic.
2. Snugly fit flank steak into a pan. Score the steak and sprinkle with salt and pepper to taste. Pour marinade over the steak. Turn to coat well. Let stand at room temperature 1 hour.
3. Broil the steak until medium done. Cutting against the grain, slice on the diagonal into 12 strips.
4. Cover crepes with mushroom spread. Place a strip of meat in the center. Fold in thirds. Put into a large baking dish.
5. Bake at 350°F 15 minutes. Serve immediately with hot Mushroom Sauce.

12 filled crepes

Cannelloni

½ pound Italian sausage, cooked and finely chopped
1 cup cooked chopped beef
1 package (10 ounces) frozen chopped spinach, thawed and well drained
¼ cup plus 2 tablespoons grated Parmesan cheese
⅛ teaspoon ground thyme
⅛ teaspoon pepper
  Salt
8 dinner crepes
½ cup Basic White Sauce (see page 84)
  Nutmeg

1. Combine sausage, beef, spinach, ¼ cup cheese, thyme, pepper, and salt to taste.
2. Divide filling among crepes. Assemble, using tube method. Top with white sauce, remaining Parmesan, and nutmeg.
3. Bake at 350°F 20 minutes.

8 filled crepes

Greek Style Beef Pie

1 pound chopped beef
2 tablespoons chopped onion
2 tablespoons ketchup
¼ teaspoon nutmeg
  Dash cinnamon
1 small eggplant (about 1 pound)
3 tablespoons oil
2 medium cloves garlic, crushed in a
  garlic press
¼ cup water
8 ounces dairy sour cream
½ cup grated Parmesan cheese
1 egg
½ teaspoon oregano
8 dinner crepes

1. Sauté beef and onion; drain. Add ketchup, nutmeg, and cinnamon; stir until well blended.
2. Pare and dice eggplant. Sauté in oil and 1 clove garlic; add water and simmer 10 to 15 minutes. Add to meat mixture.
3. Combine sour cream, 1 clove garlic, grated cheese, egg, and oregano; beat until well blended.
4. Assemble, using tart method, with the meat-eggplant mixture for the filling and the cheese mixture for the topping.
5. Bake at 375°F 10 minutes; reduce heat to 325°F and continue baking 25 minutes. Cool 5 minutes; remove from muffin pan. Serve.

8 pies

Beef with Cucumber Sauce

1 cup Dilled Cucumber Hollandaise
  (see page 84)
1 pound ground beef
¼ cup chopped onion
1 small clove garlic, crushed in a
  garlic press
2 teaspoons Worcestershire sauce
  Salt and pepper
6 dinner crepes

1. Make the hollandaise and set aside.
2. Combine beef, onion, garlic, and Worcestershire sauce. Sauté meat mixture. Drain off fat and crumble meat. Stir in ½ cup of hollandaise. Season with salt and pepper to taste.
3. Assemble, using tube method. Top with remaining sauce. Serve immediately.

6 filled crepes

Beef-Cabbage Rolls

1 pound chopped beef
⅓ cup chopped onion
1¼ cups chopped cabbage
¼ teaspoon marjoram
¼ teaspoon chili powder
  Salt and pepper
2 tablespoons flour

1. Sauté beef, onion, and 1 cup cabbage until cooked. Drain off all but 2 tablespoons of fat from mixture. Stir in marjoram and chili powder. Season with salt and pepper to taste. Stir in flour. Add 2 tomatoes, crushing them as you stir them in. Cook until beef-tomato mixture is thick.
2. Assemble, using egg-roll method. Place, seam side down, in a baking dish.

1 can (16 ounces) tomatoes in
    purée, drained;
    reserve purée
6 dinner crepes
2 teaspoons vinegar
2 teaspoons sugar

3. Bake at 375°F 15 minutes.
4. While rolls are baking, make a sauce by sautéing the remaining cabbage and tomatoes, crushed, until cabbage is tender. Add reserved purée from tomatoes, vinegar, sugar, and salt and pepper to taste; simmer 10 minutes.
5. Serve Beef-Cabbage Rolls with sauce.

6 filled crepes

Cheeseburger Crepes

1 pound ground beef
1 egg, slightly beaten
½ teaspoon seasoned salt
½ teaspoon Worcestershire sauce
⅓ cup shredded Swiss cheese
⅓ cup shredded Cheddar cheese
3 tablespoons blue cheese,
    crumbled (optional)
2 tablespoons dairy sour cream
    Pepper
6 dinner crepes
6 slices tomato
6 slices pickle

1. Combine beef, egg, seasoned salt, and Worcestershire sauce; mix until well blended.
2. Sauté meat mixture until meat is medium well done. Remove from heat. Drain off all fat. Crumble meat. Stir in cheeses and sour cream. Season with pepper to taste.
3. Assemble, using turnover method. Place on ungreased baking sheet.
4. Bake at 375°F 10 minutes.
5. Serve immediately, garnished with a slice of tomato and pickle.

6 filled crepes

Note: If desired, serve topped with Mushroom Sauce (page 88), Creamy Brown Sauce (page 89), or Rich Cheese Sauce (page 85).

Taco Crepes

1 pound ground beef
2 tablespoons chopped onion
1 can (16 ounces) tomatoes, drained
    and coarsely chopped
⅓ cup coarsely chopped green pepper
1 teaspoon salt
½ teaspoon oregano
¼ teaspoon pepper
¼ teaspoon garlic powder
1 teaspoon vinegar
8 ounces prepared taco sauce
6 dinner crepes
½ pound Cheddar cheese, coarsely
    shredded
½ cup shredded lettuce
1 large tomato, chopped

1. Sauté beef and onion until brown; stir frequently. Add tomatoes, green pepper, salt, oregano, pepper, garlic powder, vinegar, and 4 tablespoons taco sauce to meat mixture. Cook until green pepper is tender.
2. Put crepes on a baking sheet. Spoon some mixture onto half of each crepe. Fold crepe in half. Top with remaining taco sauce. Sprinkle with cheese.
3. Bake at 375°F 10 minutes.
4. Serve, topped with shredded lettuce and chopped tomato.

6 filled crepes

Creamed Chipped Beef Turnovers

1½ cups Basic White Sauce
    (see page 84)
2 hard-cooked eggs, chopped
5 ounces dried beef, rinsed
½ teaspoon Worcestershire sauce
8 ounces canned peas
8 dinner crepes

1. Make white sauce; stir in eggs, beef, and Worcestershire sauce. Cook 5 minutes. Stir in peas.
2. Assemble, using turnover method. Place on a baking sheet.
3. Bake at 350°F 15 minutes.

8 turnovers

Cheesy Beef Squares

½ pound chopped beef
¼ cup minced onion
3 tablespoons diced celery
1 medium clove garlic, crushed
¼ teaspoon rosemary
⅛ teaspoon thyme
⅛ teaspoon marjoram
2 tablespoons chopped ripe olives
2 tablespoons red wine
¼ teaspoon salt
⅛ teaspoon pepper
1 tablespoon butter or
    margarine
2 tablespoons flour
½ cup milk
⅓ cup shredded sharp Cheddar
    cheese
⅛ teaspoon nutmeg
    Dash cayenne pepper
6 dinner crepes
    Paprika

1. Sauté meat, onion, celery, garlic, rosemary, thyme, and marjoram. Add olives and red wine. Simmer until celery is tender. Drain off any liquid; add salt and pepper.
2. Make a roux with butter and flour. Gradually add milk; continue cooking until very thick. Remove from heat; stir in cheese, nutmeg, and cayenne.
3. Combine ⅓ cup of this very thick cheese sauce with meat mixture.
4. Assemble crepes, using square turnover method; use 2 to 3 tablespoons of meat mixture for filling.
5. Place meat squares on a cookie sheet, spread remaining cheese sauce on top, and sprinkle with paprika.
6. Bake at 375°F 10 minutes. Serve immediately.

6 filled crepes

Corned Beef Boiled Dinner

2 medium onions, cooked
1 carrot, cooked
2 cups chopped corned beef
½ cup cooked shredded cabbage
    Salt and pepper
2 tablespoons ketchup
8 dinner crepes

1. Chop onions and carrot. Mix with corned beef and cabbage. Add salt and pepper to taste. Stir in ketchup.
2. Assemble, using egg-roll method. Place in a baking dish, seam side down.
3. Bake at 375°F 15 minutes.

8 filled crepes

Veal Paprikash Turnovers

¼ cup butter or margarine
⅓ cup chopped onion
1½ pounds veal cutlets, cut in strips
1 teaspoon paprika
½ teaspoon salt
2 tablespoons ketchup
8 ounces dairy sour cream
6 dinner crepes

1. Melt butter; sauté onion and veal until meat is tender.
2. Stir in paprika, salt, and ketchup. Simmer 3 minutes. Stir in sour cream until well blended. Remove from heat.
3. Assemble, using turnover method. Place in a baking dish and top with remaining sauce.
4. Bake at 375°F 10 minutes. Serve immediately.

6 turnovers

Veal Madeleine

1 pound veal cutlets
3 tablespoons flour
¼ teaspoon paprika
¼ teaspoon salt
  Pinch pepper
2 tablespoons butter or margarine
3 tablespoons chopped onion
½ cup sherry
⅛ teaspoon oregano
3 dashes nutmeg
1 package (3 ounces) cream cheese, diced
6 dinner crepes
3 tablespoons shredded Swiss cheese

1. Cut veal into strips.
2. Combine flour, paprika, salt, and pepper. Dredge veal in flour mixture.
3. Melt butter. Sauté veal and onion. Stir in sherry, oregano, and nutmeg. Simmer, covered, about 30 minutes or until veal is tender. Blend in cream cheese.
4. Assemble, using tube method. Place on a baking sheet. Top with Swiss cheese.
5. Bake at 350°F 10 minutes.

6 filled crepes

Veal Cordon Bleu

¼ cup butter or margarine
1 pound thin veal cutlets, pounded and cut in short strips
2 tablespoons white wine
½ cup shredded Swiss cheese
  Salt and pepper
8 dinner crepes
¼ pound thinly sliced boiled ham
  Paprika

1. Melt butter, add veal strips, and sauté until tender. Add wine; simmer 3 minutes. Remove from heat; stir in ⅓ cup Swiss cheese. Season with salt and pepper.
2. Spread crepes out on a work surface. Divide ham slices among crepes. Spoon veal mixture onto ham. Continue assembling, using square turnover method. Place, seam side down, on a baking sheet and top with remaining cheese. Sprinkle with paprika.
3. Bake at 375°F 15 minutes. Serve piping hot.

8 filled crepes

Note: Substitute chicken for veal, if desired.

Veal, Mushrooms, and Artichokes

1½ pounds boneless veal, cut in bite-size pieces
¼ cup butter
¼ teaspoon salt
1 cup Mushroom-Garlic Spread (see page 21)
4 cooked artichoke hearts, coarsely chopped
6 dinner crepes
¼ pound Swiss cheese, coarsely shredded
½ cup white wine
2 tablespoons ketchup

1. Sauté veal in butter. Reduce heat and add salt. Cook covered for 15 minutes, or until tender.
2. Combine ½ cup mushroom spread and chopped artichoke hearts.
3. Spread mixture over the crepes. Place meat on half of crepe and fold. Put on a baking sheet. Sprinkle with cheese.
4. Bake at 400°F 3 to 4 minutes, or until cheese melts. Add wine, ketchup, and remaining mushroom spread to the pan drippings from the veal. Stirring constantly, simmer gently 1 minute.
5. Serve on hot plates with sauce spooned over the top of the crepe.

6 servings

Note: Chicken can be substituted for the veal.

Lebanese Lamb Turnovers

1 pound lamb (in small cubes)
¼ cup oil
2 medium cloves garlic, crushed in a press
1 cup chopped onion
1 can (16 ounces) tomatoes (undrained)
1 teaspoon thyme
¼ teaspoon cinnamon
1 medium eggplant (1 pound), pared and diced
2 tablespoons raisins
2 tablespoons pinenuts
16 dinner crepes

1. Sauté lamb in oil until tender (7 to 10 minutes). Stir in garlic and onion and cook until onion is tender. Add tomatoes and juice, thyme, cinnamon, and eggplant. Simmer until eggplant is tender, about 15 minutes.
2. Add raisins and pinenuts. Continue to simmer until sauce is reduced to half its volume.
3. Assemble, using turnover method. Place on a baking sheet.
4. Bake at 375°F 10 minutes.
5. Keep remaining sauce warm. Serve topped with remaining sauce.

16 turnovers

Moussaka Tarts

½ pound ground lamb
2 tablespoons ketchup
¼ teaspoon nutmeg
2 tablespoons minced onion
Dash cinnamon
1 small eggplant (about 1 pound)
3 tablespoons oil
2 medium cloves garlic, crushed in a garlic press
¼ cup water
1 cup ricotta cheese
½ cup grated Parmesan cheese
1 egg

1. Simmer lamb, ketchup, nutmeg, onion, and cinnamon until meat and onion are tender.
2. While the meat is simmering, pare and dice the eggplant. Sauté eggplant in oil. Stir in 1 clove garlic and water; simmer until eggplant is tender but firm.
3. To make the cheese topping, combine ricotta, 1 clove of garlic, grated cheese, and egg.
4. Assemble, using tart method; use the lamb mixture as the first layer, eggplant as the second, and cheese as the third.
5. Bake at 375°F 10 minutes. Turn oven control to 325°F and continue baking for 25 minutes. Cool 5 minutes before removing from pan.

8 tarts

Oriental Pork Turnovers

½ pound pork, cut in strips
⅛ teaspoon ginger
1/16 teaspoon dry mustard
1 teaspoon brown sugar
2 dashes salt
1 tablespoon soy sauce
2 tablespoons oil
¼ cup duck sauce (sweet and sour)
4 dinner crepes

1. Marinate pork strips in a mixture of ginger, mustard, brown sugar, salt, and soy sauce 30 minutes.
2. Drain and sauté in oil until tender. Stir 2 tablespoons of sauce into pork strips.
3. Assemble, using turnover method. Brush remaining sauce on top of each turnover. Place on a baking sheet.
4. Bake at 375°F 10 minutes. Serve piping hot with sautéed oriental vegetables, if desired.

4 turnovers

Note: Substitute chicken for pork, if desired.

Beef Stroganoff Turnovers, 26

Pork and Broccoli

½ pound pork, cut in strips
1 tablespoon vinegar
1 package (10 ounces) chopped broccoli, thawed and drained
2 tablespoons oil
2 tablespoons butter or margarine
¼ cup chopped onion
1 medium clove garlic, crushed
¼ teaspoon dried basil
1 cup light cream or half-and-half
1½ teaspoons arrowroot
1 can (about 10 ounces) condensed cream of mushroom soup
8 dinner crepes

1. Marinate pork in vinegar 30 minutes. Drain.
2. Sauté pork and broccoli in oil until both are tender.
3. For sauce, melt butter, sauté onion, garlic, and basil. Add cream, arrowroot, and mushroom soup; stir until smooth. Bring to boiling; remove from heat.
4. Blend ¾ cup sauce into pork-broccoli mixture. Assemble, using square turnover method. Arrange on a baking sheet.
5. Bake at 375°F 15 minutes. Serve, topped with remaining sauce.

8 filled crepes

Note: If desired, substitute veal or lamb for pork and omit vinegar.

Pork Barbecue Turnovers

2 cups pork strips
¾ cup Barbecue Sauce (see page 86)
6 dinner crepes
½ cup shredded Cheddar cheese

1. Sauté pork strips. Stir in ½ cup sauce. Simmer 5 minutes.
2. Assemble, using turnover method. Brush tops with remaining sauce. Top with cheese.
3. Bake at 375°F 15 minutes.

6 turnovers

Beef Barbecue Turnovers: Follow recipe for Pork Barbecue Turnovers; omit pork. Brown **1 pound ground beef** and drain before adding sauce.

Tongue Rolls with Spinach Topping

½ pound cooked tongue, chopped
⅓ cup mayonnaise
1½ teaspoons prepared horseradish
6 dinner crepes
¾ cup Basic White Sauce (see page 84)
¼ cup cooked spinach, drained

1. Combine tongue, mayonnaise, and horseradish. Spread on crepes; roll up jelly-roll fashion. Place rolls in a baking dish.
2. Combine white sauce and spinach. Spread over the top of the rolls.
3. Bake at 350°F 15 minutes. Serve immediately.

6 rolls

Note: Rolls without topping can be cut into thirds and served as a snack.

Tongue Rolls with Dilled Spinach Topping: Follow recipe for Tongue Rolls with Spinach Topping. Substitute **Dilled Cucumber Hollandaise** (see page 84) for white sauce and combine with spinach for topping.

Chicken Italiano, 38

Ham Foldovers

1½ cups Basic White Sauce (page 84)
1 tablespoon Dijon mustard
1 pound cooked ham, cut in ¼-inch cubes
½ pound American cheese, cut in ¼-inch cubes
1 can (16 ounces) green peas, drained
8 dinner crepes
¼ pound Swiss cheese, coarsely shredded

1. Prepare sauce. Reserve ½ cup of sauce for topping.
2. To the remaining sauce, add mustard, ham, American cheese, and peas. Mix gently.
3. Divide filling among crepes. Fold crepes in half. Put on a baking sheet. Spread reserved sauce over tops of crepes and sprinkle with Swiss cheese.
4. Bake at 350°F 15 minutes. Serve at once.

8 filled crepes

Sausage Foldovers: Follow recipe for Ham Foldovers; substitute **1 pound cooked Italian sausage** for ham.

Ham Logs with Raisin Sauce

1 can (4½ ounces) deviled ham spread
1 tablespoon mayonnaise
¼ teaspoon dry mustard
4 dinner crepes
¼ cup raisins
½ cup water
1 teaspoon vinegar
1 tablespoon brown sugar
1 teaspoon cornstarch
¹/₁₆ teaspoon cinnamon

1. Combine ham spread, mayonnaise, and mustard. Spread on crepes. Roll up jelly-roll fashion. Place roll on a baking sheet, seam side down.
2. Bake at 375°F 10 minutes.
3. While they are baking, make sauce. Simmer raisins in water until plumped. Stir in vinegar and brown sugar and cook until sugar dissolves. Add cornstarch and cook, stirring constantly, until thickened. Stir in cinnamon.
4. Top hot ham logs with sauce. Serve immediately.

4 logs

Pork with Yam Sauce

1 pound boneless lean pork
5 tablespoons butter or margarine
6 tablespoons flour
1½ cups milk
3 beef bouillon cubes
¾ cup hot water
¼ teaspoon ginger
⅛ teaspoon thyme
1 medium clove garlic
1½ cups coarsely mashed canned yams (packed in heavy syrup)

1. Dice pork into bite-size pieces. Sauté in 2 tablespoons butter or margarine until tender. Reserve meat.
2. For sauce, melt remaining butter and stir in flour. Gradually add milk, stirring until smooth. Dissolve bouillon cubes in hot water and stir into sauce. Cook and stir until smooth and thick. Add ginger, thyme, garlic, and yams. (Sauce should be pale orange and thick with pieces of yam in it.)
3. Combine half of the sauce with meat and divide among crepes. Fold each crepe in half. Place on a baking sheet; top with remaining sauce.
4. Bake at 375°F 10 minutes. Serve hot.

6 filled crepes

Tropical Ham au Gratin

¾ **pound boiled ham, cut in cubes**
2 **small bananas, diced**
¼ **teaspoon dry mustard**
½ **cup shredded Cheddar cheese**
12 **dinner crepes**

1. Sauté ham and banana until warm. Stir in mustard. Remove from heat. Stir in cheese.
2. Assemble, using square turnover method. Place on baking sheet.
3. Bake at 375°F 5 minutes. Serve hot. This can be served as a snack.

12 filled crepes

Peking Crepes

A Peking Crepe is not your run-of-the-mill crepe recipe. It is actually assembled by individuals, at the table, to their taste. Explain to the people how it is done and what is on the platter to choose from. Caution them not to overfill the crepes and to eat them like a sandwich. Children and adults really enjoy this dish.

1½ **cups shredded cooked meat (any combination of roast pork, roast beef, chicken, turkey, duck, ham, or bacon)**
1 **cucumber, pared and very thinly sliced**
3 **whole scallions, coarsely chopped**
½ **cup duck sauce (sweet and sour) or ketchup**
1 **egg, beaten**
1 **tablespoon butter or margarine**
3 **tablespoons oil**
1 **cup bean sprouts**
3 **tablespoons soy sauce**
1½ **cups shredded cabbage**
12 **dinner crepes**

1. Arrange meat, cucumber, and scallions in separate mounds on a large serving platter. Put duck sauce in bowl in center.
2. Make an omelet with the egg and butter. Cool and cut into thin strips. Mound on the platter.
3. Heat 1 tablespoon of oil; add bean sprouts and fry 5 minutes, stirring constantly. Season with 1 tablespoon of soy sauce. Mound on the platter.
4. Heat remaining oil and soy sauce. Add cabbage. Stir-fry 5 minutes. Mound on platter.
5. Stack crepes on another plate.
6. To serve, have guests spread crepe with sauce, top with meat and vegetables, about 2 tablespoons total. *Do not overfill.* Fold in half and then in quarters. Eat as a sandwich.

12 filled crepes

Jambalaya

¼ **cup minced green pepper**
¼ **cup minced onion**
½ **cup diced celery**
3 **tablespoons oil**
1 **cup minced cooked chicken**
1 **cup minced cooked ham**
1 **cup minced cooked Italian sausage**
1 **can (8 ounces) tomato sauce**
1 **teaspoon chili powder**
8 **dinner crepes**

1. Sauté green pepper, onion, and celery in oil. Stir in chicken, ham, and sausage.
2. Combine tomato sauce and chili powder. Stir ¾ cup sauce into meat mixture.
3. Assemble, using tube method. Put into a baking dish. Top with remaining sauce.
4. Bake at 375°F 10 minutes.

8 filled crepes

Pizza Tarts

1 pound Italian sausage, chopped
¼ pound mushrooms, cleaned and chopped
¼ cup chopped green pepper
1 clove garlic, crushed in a garlic press
¼ cup chopped onion
½ teaspoon oregano
12 dinner crepes
¾ cup shredded mozzarella cheese
⅓ cup grated Parmesan cheese
¾ cup warm tomato sauce

1. Sauté sausage, mushrooms, pepper, garlic, onion, and oregano until meat is cooked. Drain and cool.
2. Using 2 tablespoons sausage-vegetable mixture as first filling, 1 tablespoon mozzarella for second layer, and 1½ teaspoons Parmesan cheese as topping, assemble, using tart method.
3. Bake at 325°F 30 minutes.
4. About 5 minutes before tarts are finished baking, heat tomato sauce.
5. Cool tarts 5 minutes. Remove from muffin pans. Top with warm sauce and remaining grated cheese. Serve warm.

12 tarts

Note: Anchovy fillets may be added, one per tart.

Franks and Beans

½ cup Barbecue Sauce (see page 86)
2 teaspoons dry mustard
2 cans (16 ounces each) vegetarian beans or pork and beans
8 dinner crepes
1 pound frankfurters (8 to a pound)

1. Combine sauce and mustard. Drain and mash beans. Combine beans and sauce.
2. Spread bean mixture on crepes. Place the frankfurter on one edge of the crepe and roll up. Place on a baking sheet.
3. Bake at 375°F 15 minutes.

8 filled crepes

Note: Top with drained sauerkraut, if desired.

Cheesy Franks and Beans: Follow recipe for Franks and Beans. Place a **strip of cheese** inside crepe with frankfurter. After crepe has baked 10 minutes, place a strip of cheese on top and continue baking 5 minutes.

POULTRY

Chicken Italiano

2 whole chicken breasts (about 1 pound)
2 tablespoons oil
½ pound mushrooms, cleaned and chopped
1 can (16 ounces) stewed tomatoes
1 medium clove garlic, crushed in a garlic press
1 teaspoon oregano
½ teaspoon thyme
1 can (8 ounces) tomato sauce
⅓ cup grated Parmesan cheese
Salt and pepper
6 dinner crepes

1. Bone chicken and cut into 1-inch strips.
2. Heat oil, sauté chicken and mushrooms until chicken turns white. Stir in stewed tomatoes, garlic, oregano, thyme, tomato sauce, and 3 tablespoons grated cheese. Add salt and pepper to taste. Simmer, uncovered, 5 minutes.
3. Using a slotted spoon, spoon onto crepes. Assemble, using tube method, place on a baking sheet, and sprinkle tops of crepes with remaining cheese.
4. Bake at 375°F until cheese browns (about 15 minutes) Serve immediately with any remaining sauce.

6 filled crepes

Creamed Chicken

3 tablespoons butter or margarine
¼ cup flour
1 tablespoon chopped parsley
¼ teaspoon dried tarragon
1½ cups whipping cream
2 cups diced cooked chicken
Salt and pepper
6 dinner crepes
Paprika

1. Melt butter (do not brown); stir in flour. Add parsley, tarragon, and cream. Cook until thick. Add chicken and salt and pepper to taste.
2. Divide among crepes. Fold in half; place on a baking sheet. Sprinkle with paprika.
3. Bake at 375°F 15 minutes.

6 filled crepes

Curried Chicken Salad in Butterfly Crepes

1 chicken (2½ pounds), cut in pieces
1 bay leaf
1 teaspoon thyme
½ teaspoon salt
Boiling water
¼ cup mayonnaise
¼ teaspoon curry powder
¼ teaspoon poultry seasoning
2 teaspoons curry powder
2 tablespoons chutney
⅔ cup dairy sour cream

1. Place chicken, bay leaf, thyme, and salt in a deep saucepan and cover with boiling water. Cover. Simmer, do not boil, 1 hour, or until tender.
2. While chicken is simmering, combine mayonnaise and ¼ teaspoon curry powder. Cover. Chill.
3. Remove skin and bones from chicken. Finely dice chicken; cool.
4. Mix cool chicken, poultry seasoning, remaining curry powder, and chutney. Add sour cream and mix until all ingredients are moist and mixture holds its shape. Add salt and pepper to taste.
5. Assemble crepes using butterfly method, with chicken salad

Salt and pepper
6 dinner crepes
  Chopped peanuts or cashews
  Flaked coconut
2 spiced peaches, cut in 8 wedges

for filling and topping. Garnish wings by dotting with curried mayonnaise and sprinkling with chopped nuts and coconut. Form antennae with peach wedges. Serve at room temperature.

4 servings

Note: Salad may be made in advance and stored in refrigerator until ready to assemble.

Mandarin Chicken Turnovers

1 chicken (2½ pounds)
2 scallions, minced
⅓ cup diced celery
¼ cup butter or margarine
1 can (11 ounces) mandarin
    oranges, drained; reserve
    syrup
2 teaspoons soy sauce
  Dash cayenne pepper
⅛ teaspoon minced crystallized
    ginger
2 teaspoons cornstarch
8 dinner crepes

1. Skin, bone, and dice chicken.
2. Sauté chicken, scallions, and celery in butter until chicken is cooked.
3. Make mandarin sauce by adding water to reserved syrup, if necessary, to equal ⅔ cup liquid. Combine this liquid with soy sauce, cayenne, ginger, and cornstarch. Stir until well blended. Cook, stirring constantly, over medium heat until mixture turns clear and thickens. Stir in mandarin oranges.
4. Stir half the sauce into hot sautéed chicken.
5. Assemble, using turnover method.
6. Serve immediately, topped with remaining sauce; or for a crispy crepe, place on a baking sheet and bake at 375°F 10 minutes. Serve immediately with remaining warm sauce.

8 turnovers

Sicilian Chicken

1 pound boned chicken
1 package (10 ounces) frozen
    chopped broccoli, thawed
2 tablespoons oil
¼ pound mushrooms, cleaned and
    sliced
⅔ cup Pesto Sauce (see page 88)
8 dinner crepes
½ cup Basic White Sauce (see page 84)
  Parsley

1. Cut chicken into 1×¼-inch strips. Drain broccoli.
2. Heat oil and sauté chicken, mushrooms, and broccoli until tender. Drain off any liquid; stir in Pesto Sauce.
3. Assemble, using square turnover method. Place on a baking sheet, separating slightly; top with white sauce.
4. Bake at 375°F 10 minutes. Serve garnished with parsley.

8 filled crepes

Chicken and Shrimp Egg Roll

- 3 tablespoons oil
- ½ pound raw chicken, cut in julienne strips *
- ½ pound shrimp, cleaned and diced
- 1 can (16 ounces) bean sprouts, well drained
- ⅓ cup coarsely chopped celery
- 8 scallions, thinly sliced
- ½ cup shredded cabbage
- 1 tablespoon soy sauce
- 1 teaspoon salt
- 12 dinner crepes
  Oil for frying

1. Heat 3 tablespoons oil in skillet. Sauté chicken, stirring frequently. Add shrimp, bean sprouts, celery, scallions, and cabbage. Cook 4 minutes. Season with soy sauce and salt. Cool 10 minutes.
2. Assemble, using egg-roll method.
3. Fry in ⅛ inch heated oil in a skillet until golden. Serve hot.

12 egg rolls

Note: Egg rolls can be stored in the refrigerator or freezer. To reheat, bake at 375°F 15 minutes.

*If desired, use all chicken or all shrimp, or substitute pork for chicken.

Chicken Curry Turnovers

- 1 chicken (2½ pounds)
- 2½ tablespoons Curry Powder
- 3 tablespoons butter or margarine
- ½ cup chopped onion
- ¾ cup unsweetened applesauce
- 2 tablespoons Peach Chutney (see page 89)
  Salt and pepper
- 6 dinner crepes

1. Skin, bone, and dice chicken. Toss chicken with Curry Powder.
2. Sauté coated chicken in butter with onion until tender. Stir in applesauce and chutney. Simmer 10 minutes.
3. Assemble, using turnover method.
4. Bake at 375°F 10 minutes.
5. Serve with Condiments for Curry.

6 turnovers

Curry Powder: Put **1 teaspoon cumin seed, 2 teaspoons coriander seed, 2½ tablespoons sesame seed, 2 teaspoons turmeric, ½ teaspoon chili powder, ¼ teaspoon ground ginger, ¼ teaspoon garlic powder,** and **1 teaspoon salt** into an electric blender container. Blend at medium-high speed until well blended and a powder. Store in a tightly covered container.

⅓ cup powder

Condiments for Curry: **Chutney, chopped peanuts or cashews, chopped green pepper, flaked coconut, diced bananas, chopped raisins, quartered kumquats, sliced scallions, shredded cucumber, crushed or chunk pineapple, yogurt, diced apple, diced banana,** or **crumbled bacon.**

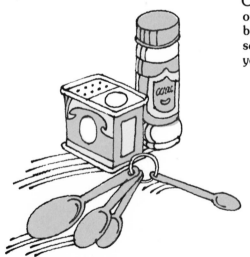

Chicken Liver and Green Grape Turnovers

1 pound chicken livers
¼ cup butter or margarine
2 tablespoons minced onion
¼ teaspoon salt
⅛ teaspoon ginger
⅛ teaspoon pepper
1 teaspoon Worcestershire sauce
1 cup seedless green grapes, cut in half
1 tablespoon sherry
1 chicken bouillon cube
¼ cup water
⅓ cup dairy sour cream
2 tablespoons chopped parsley
8 dinner crepes

1. Sauté chicken livers in butter 3 minutes. Stir in onion and sauté 4 minutes more.
2. Add salt, ginger, pepper, Worcestershire sauce, grapes, sherry, bouillon cube, and water. Simmer 3 minutes. Remove from heat. Stir in sour cream and parsley.
3. Assemble, using turnover method.
4. Bake at 350°F 10 minutes. Serve immediately.

8 turnovers

Chicken Polynesian Turnovers

2 chicken breasts, boned (about 1 pound)
¼ cup bottled teriyaki sauce
¼ cup oil
1 large banana, diced
1 can (8 ounces) crushed pineapple, drained; reserve juice
¼ cup chopped green pepper
1 tablespoon honey
1 tablespoon soy sauce
1 tablespoon cornstarch
4 dinner crepes

1. Cut boned chicken breasts into short strips. Marinate in teriyaki sauce for 20 minutes.
2. Heat oil; sauté chicken until tender. Stir in diced banana, crushed pineapple, and green pepper. Simmer 3 to 5 minutes to heat fruit.
3. Assemble, using turnover method. Place on a baking sheet.
4. Bake at 375°F 15 minutes.
5. While crepes are baking, make a sauce with ½ cup reserved pineapple juice, honey, soy sauce, and cornstarch; cook until mixture thickens.
6. Serve hot crepes with sauce on top. Accompany with stir-fried vegetables, if desired.

4 turnovers

Turkey-Asparagus Turnovers

Mushroom Cheese Spread (see Pinwheel Party Platter, page 16)
8 dinner crepes
8 slices (1 ounce each) turkey breast
24 asparagus spears, cooked
Paprika

1. Prepare Mushroom Cheese Spread; reserve half the spread for topping. Spread remaining mixture over crepes. Top with one slice of turkey and three asparagus spears. Fold in half. Put onto a baking sheet. Top with reserved spread; sprinkle with paprika.
2. Bake at 375°F 10 minutes.

8 turnovers

Ham-Green Bean Turnovers: Follow recipe for Turkey-Asparagus Turnovers, substituting **ham** for turkey and **whole green beans** for asparagus.

Turkey Divan

1 package (10 ounces) frozen
    broccoli spears
½ cup Lemon Sauce (see page 88)
¾ pound cooked white turkey meat
4 dinner crepes
2 tablespoons grated Parmesan
    cheese
    Paprika

1. Cook broccoli following directions on package. Drain.
2. Prepare Lemon Sauce.
3. Cut turkey into julienne strips. Spread 1 tablespoon of lemon sauce over each crepe. On lower half place broccoli and turkey. Fold crepe in half.
4. Put into a baking dish. Spread remaining sauce over top of crepes. Sprinkle with cheese and then with paprika.
5. Bake at 375°F 15 minutes.

4 servings

Turkey à la King

2 tablespoons butter or margarine
¼ cup chopped onion
¼ pound mushrooms, cleaned and
    sliced
1½ cups Basic White Sauce (see
    page 84)
½ teaspoon Worcestershire sauce
1½ tablespoons chopped pimento
6 dinner crepes
1 cup diced cooked turkey

1. Melt butter. Sauté onion and mushrooms until tender. Stir in white sauce, Worcestershire sauce, and pimento. Simmer 5 minutes.
2. To assemble, spread crepe with some sauce, divide turkey among crepes, and proceed, using turnover method.
3. Bake at 375°F 10 minutes.
4. Keep remaining sauce warm. Serve crepes topped with remaining sauce.

6 filled crepes

Note: Substitute 1 cup diced cooked chicken, pork, or veal for turkey, if desired.

FISH
AND SEAFOOD

Lobster Newburg

¼ cup butter or margarine
6 tablespoons flour
1½ cups light cream
1 tablespoon cooking liquid from lobster (if possible)
3 tablespoons sherry
¼ teaspoon nutmeg
3 dashes cayenne pepper
Pinch of paprika
1 egg yolk, slightly beaten
1 egg white
2 cups cubed, cooked lobster
12 dinner crepes

1. Melt butter, stir in flour, and cook 1 minute. Slowly stir in light cream and liquid from lobster. Cook, stirring continuously, until smooth and thick.
2. Blend in sherry, nutmeg, cayenne, and paprika. Slowly add egg yolk, blend well, and cook until smooth and thick (about 3 minutes).
3. Combine half of the sauce with the lobster meat. Reserve the rest.
4. To assemble, place a heaping tablespoon of the lobster mixture on one quarter of the crepe. Brush remaining three quarters of crepe with egg white. Fold into cone-shaped packages. Place in baking dish, one cone overlapping the other, with the open part of the cone upward.
5. Bake at 375°F 10 minutes. Serve 2 for an appetizer or 3 for dinner, topped with warmed remaining sauce.

12 filled crepes

Lobster Duxelles: Sauté **½ pound sliced mushrooms** in **1 tablespoon butter or margarine** and add to the sauce. This will increase yield to fill 15 crepes.

Crab Newburg: Substitute **2 cups cooked, flaked crab** for lobster.

Shrimp Newburg: Sauté **⅓ cup minced celery** and **¼ pound sliced mushrooms** in **2 tablespoons butter or margarine**. Substitute **celery, mushrooms,** and **1½ cups cooked shrimp** for lobster.

Scallop Newburg: Sauté **¼ pound sliced mushrooms** and **2 tablespoons snipped parsley** in **1 tablespoon butter.** Substitute **mushrooms, parsley,** and **2 cups scallops** for lobster. This will increase the filling yield slightly, so fill each crepe with 2 level tablespoons scallop mixture.

Lobster Thermidor Turnovers

½ cup white wine
2 tablespoons minced onion
½ cup chicken stock
3 tablespoons butter or margarine
4 tablespoons flour
1 cup light cream or half-and-half
¾ cup grated Parmesan cheese
¼ teaspoon thyme
½ pound fresh white mushrooms, sliced
2 cups cooked lobster, cubed*
8 dinner crepes

1. Combine wine, onion, and chicken stock in a saucepan. Simmer until reduced to half; set aside.
2. In a large skillet make a roux with butter and flour. Gradually add cream; stir until smooth.
3. Cook over medium heat, stirring constantly, until thick.
4. Stir wine mixture into skillet; simmer 5 minutes.
5. Stir in ½ cup cheese, thyme, and mushrooms; simmer 5 minutes.
6. Add lobster; continue cooking 3 minutes.
7. Assemble, using turnover method; place on broiler pan, and sprinkle with remaining cheese.
8. Broil until cheese browns. Serve immediately.

8 turnovers

*Any cooked seafood (shrimp, crab, scallops) or fish can be substituted.

Lobster Diablo

2 tablespoons butter or margarine
2 cups diced lobster meat
1 can (16 ounces) tomatoes, drained
½ medium onion, chopped
½ teaspoon oregano
½ teaspoon minced fresh parsley
1 medium clove garlic, crushed
¼ cup chopped ripe olives
2 drops Tabasco
8 dinner crepes

1. Melt butter in skillet. Sauté lobster in butter until cooked, then remove lobster from skillet.
2. Crush tomatoes and add them with onion, oregano, parsley, garlic, olives, and Tabasco to the melted butter. Simmer 20 minutes.
3. Stir in sautéed lobster. Assemble, using square turnover method, putting sauce in crepes with a slotted spoon.
4. Place packets in baking dish; top with sauce.
5. Bake at 375°F 10 minutes.

8 squares

Note: Shrimp or scallops may substituted for lobster.

Jamaican Lobster Turnovers

2 tablespoons butter or margarine
2 tablespoons minced green pepper
2 tablespoons minced onion
4 tablespoons flour
1 can (16 ounces) tomatoes
10 ounces cooked lobster
2 tablespoons chopped, stuffed green olives
½ teaspoon marjoram
1½ teaspoons sugar
Salt and pepper to taste
8 dinner crepes

1. Melt butter; sauté green pepper and onion until tender. Stir in flour.
2. Break up tomatoes; add tomato pulp and juice to pepper and onion mixture. Cook until sauce thickens.
3. Cut lobster into bite-size pieces. Add lobster, olives, marjoram, and sugar to tomato mixture. Simmer for 5 minutes.
4. Add salt and pepper to taste. Assemble, using turnover method; place on baking sheet.
5. Bake at 375°F 15 minutes.

8 turnovers

Pesto Crab Squares

1 pound ricotta cheese
2 eggs, slightly beaten
1 teaspoon oregano
1 medium clove garlic, crushed
2 tablespoons grated Parmesan cheese
⅓ cup Pesto Sauce (see page 88)
6 ounces frozen king crab, drained well
12 dinner crepes
1 cup Basic White Sauce (see page 84)
Nutmeg

1. Beat ricotta cheese and eggs until smooth. Stir in oregano, garlic, Parmesan cheese, Pesto Sauce, and crab.
2. Assemble, using square turnover method. Arrange in baking dish so crepes are just touching. Top with Basic White Sauce; sprinkle with nutmeg.
3. Bake at 375°F 20 minutes. Cool 5 minutes before serving. Serve 1 for an appetizer; 2 for a dinner.

12 squares

Crab-Asparagus Supreme

1 package (10 ounces) frozen
   asparagus spears or 12 to 16
   fresh asparagus spears
1 package (6 ounces) frozen crab
   meat
2 cups Rich Cheese Sauce (page
   85)
8 dinner crepes

1. Cook asparagus spears; drain.
2. Drain and flake crab meat; mix with ½ cup Cheddar Cheese Sauce.
3. Spread 1 heaping tablespoon crab mixture in a line down center of each crepe. Place 2 small or 1 large asparagus spears on top of crab and roll crepe.
4. Place in a shallow baking dish; pour remaining sauce over top.
5. Bake at 375°F 20 minutes.

8 filled crepes

Curried Crab Florentine

3 tablespoons butter or margarine
2 cans (7½ ounces each)
   Alaska king crab meat, drained
   Salt to taste
1 scallion, chopped
1 can (4 ounces) sliced
   mushrooms, drained
1 teaspoon curry powder
   Dash cayenne pepper
   Dash Worcestershire sauce
1 tablespoon chutney (peach
   chutney may be used, see
   page 89)
1 cup Creamy Lemon Sauce (see
   page 89)
8 dinner crepes
¼ cup flaked coconut

1. Melt butter, add crab, salt (if necessary), scallion, mushrooms, curry powder, cayenne, and Worcestershire sauce.
2. Sauté until scallions are tender and mixture is thoroughly heated. Remove from heat.
3. Stir in chutney and ¼ cup Creamy Lemon Sauce. Divide mixture among crepes and assemble, using tube method.
4. Arrange snugly in a baking dish. Top with remaining sauce and sprinkle on coconut.
5. Broil about 5 inches from source of heat 3 minutes or until lightly browned.

8 filled crepes

Crab Cannelloni

1 pound ricotta or cottage cheese
1 egg, slightly beaten
¼ cup grated Parmesan cheese
1 teaspoon oregano
¼ teaspoon ground thyme
1 medium clove garlic, crushed
1 teaspoon butter or margarine
2 tablespoons minced onion
½ cup diced broccoli
6 ounces frozen king crab meat,
   drained and crumbled
10 dinner crepes
1 cup Basic White Sauce (see page
   84)
   Nutmeg

1. Beat ricotta or cottage cheese until smooth.
2. Blend in egg, Parmesan cheese, oregano, thyme, and garlic.
3. Melt butter or margarine; sauté onion and broccoli until tender; drain well.
4. Stir onion, broccoli, and crab into cheese mixture. Assemble, using tube method; fit snugly into a baking dish.
5. Bake at 350°F 20 minutes. Cool for 5 minutes. Serve topped with warm white sauce and sprinkled with nutmeg.

10 filled crepes

Crab and Mushroom Turnovers

1 small green pepper, seeded,
  cut in thin strips
1 whole pimento, cut in thin
  strips
¼ cup butter
1 pound mushrooms, cleaned
  and sliced
1 tablespoon lemon juice
½ teaspoon salt
2 cups light cream or
  half-and-half
2 packages (6 ounces each)
  frozen crab meat, drained and
  flaked (reserve liquid)
2 tablespoons butter
3 tablespoons flour
¼ cup shredded Swiss or
  grated Parmesan cheese

1. Sauté pepper and pimento strips in butter 5 minutes. Stir in mushrooms and lemon juice; cook 2 minutes. Add salt, cream, and crab liquid; bring to boiling.
2. In a large saucepan, make a roux of butter and flour. Slowly add vegetable and cream mixture to roux, stirring constantly. Cook until thickened, stirring constantly.
3. Stir in crab meat. Simmer for 1 to 2 minutes.
4. Assemble, using turnover method; sprinkle with cheese.
5. Broil for 2 minutes or until browned.

12 turnovers

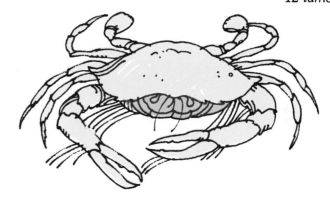

Crab à la King

¼ cup minced onion
¼ pound mushrooms, cleaned
  and sliced
2 tablespoons butter or
  margarine
1½ cups Basic White Sauce (see
  page 84)
1½ teaspoons Worcestershire sauce
1 tablespoon chopped pimento
1 teaspoon lemon juice
6 ounces frozen crab meat,
  flaked
4 dinner crepes

1. Sauté onion and mushrooms in butter until tender; stir into Basic White Sauce.
2. Add Worcestershire sauce, pimento, and lemon juice to white sauce mixture; blend well.
3. Simmer 3 minutes to blend flavors. Stir ½ cup sauce into crab meat.
4. Assemble, using tube method. Place in baking pan; top with remaining sauce.
5. Bake at 375°F 15 minutes. Serve piping hot.

4 filled crepes

Coral Shrimp

½ cup finely chopped onion
1 tablespoon butter or margarine
2 cups Basic White Sauce (see
  page 84)
1 to 2 teaspoons tomato paste
¼ cup dry white wine
½ teaspoon salt
¼ teaspoon white pepper
1 pound cooked medium shrimp
  (fresh or frozen)

1. Sauté onion in butter until tender. Mix onion into white sauce. Stir in tomato paste, wine, salt, and pepper. Fold in shrimp.
2. Assemble, using tube method. Spoon extra sauce over crepes. Garnish with **fresh tomato** and **Bibb lettuce.**

12 filled crepes

Garlic Shrimp Squares

6 ounces frozen tiny cooked shrimp

5½ ounces herbed cheese (such as tartare, Boursin, or Alouette) or ¾ cup herbed cheese spread, at room temperature (see Herbed Cheese Log, page 19)

1. Thaw shrimp, drain, and dice.
2. Blend shrimp with cheese; assemble, using square turnover method.
3. Bake at 375°F 15 minutes. Serve piping hot.

6 squares

Garlic Shrimp Pinwheels: Use filling for Garlic Shrimp Squares. Spread open crepes with filling. Broil open for 2 to 3 minutes about 5 inches from source of heat. Watch closely so they do not burn. Remove from broiler, roll up, and serve.

6 filled crepes

Note: For appetizer-size pinwheels, cool rolled crepes slightly; slice each roll into 6 pieces.

36 appetizers

Shrimp Quickie

1 can (about 10 ounces) condensed cream of mushroom soup

1 package (8 ounces) cream cheese, cubed

1 tablespoon prepared horseradish

½ teaspoon Worcestershire sauce Dash Tabasco

3 cans (4½ ounces each) tiny shrimp or 1 pound frozen shrimp, cooked and chopped

1 can (6 ounces) water chestnuts, drained and chopped

8 dinner crepes Parsley

1. Combine soup and cream cheese. Cook over medium heat, stirring until well blended. Stir in horseradish, Worcestershire sauce, and Tabasco. Remove from heat.
2. Rinse canned shrimp, drain thoroughly, and mix along with water chestnuts into the sauce. Divide filling among crepes. Fold in half. Put into a baking dish.
3. Bake at 375°F 10 minutes. Serve immediately, sprinkled with parsley.

8 filled crepes

Shrimp in Spanish Cream

2 tablespoons minced green onion or scallion (white part only)

½ cup minced onion

½ cup diced celery

¼ cup butter or margarine

½ cup dry white wine

1. Sauté onion and celery in butter in a skillet 3 to 4 minutes; stir occasionally. Add wine, tomato sauce, bay leaf, salt, and pepper to the onion mixture. Bring to boiling. Simmer 10 minutes.
2. Cook shrimp following directions on package; drain and rinse, cleaning if necessary.

1 cup tomato sauce
1 small bay leaf
½ teaspoon salt
  Dash pepper
1 pound frozen medium-size raw
  shrimp
½ cup whipping cream
  Salt and pepper
6 dinner crepes

3. Remove bay leaf from the tomato sauce. Stir in cream and simmer 8 minutes to reduce liquid. Add salt and pepper to taste. Stir in shrimp; simmer 1 minute.
4. Divide the shrimp filling among the crepes, reserving some sauce for topping. Fold each crepe in half, put into a baking dish, and top with reserved sauce.
5. Bake at 375°F 10 minutes.

6 filled crepes

Note: If desired, substitute scallops for shrimp.

Louisiana Shrimp Salad

1 package (6 ounces) frozen tiny
  cooked shrimp
1 small tomato, diced
1 hard-cooked egg, diced
3 tablespoons chopped ripe olives
1 scallion, finely chopped
  Salt and pepper to taste
⅓ cup dairy sour cream
¼ cup chili sauce
4 dinner crepes
  Garnish: parsley, sliced tomato,
    ripe olives

1. Combine shrimp, tomato, egg, olives, and scallion. Sprinkle salt and pepper over mixture.
2. For dressing, blend sour cream with chili sauce.
3. Toss shrimp and vegetables with dressing.
4. Assemble, using tube method. Place on individual plates, garnish, and serve.

4 filled crepes

Shrimp Curry

1 tablespoon butter or margarine
3 ounces cream cheese, softened
2 teaspoons chunky peanut butter
1 teaspoon Curry Powder (see
  page 40)
1 pound frozen shrimp, cooked,
  cleaned, and diced
6 dinner crepes
  Condiments for Curry (see page
    40)

1. Melt butter in saucepan. Blend in cream cheese, peanut butter, and Curry Powder. Stir over heat until well blended.
2. Stir shrimp into sauce. Assemble, using tube method; place in baking dish.
3. Bake at 350°F 15 minutes. Serve with assortment of Condiments for Curry.

6 filled crepes

Crab-Avocado Curry: Substitute **7½ ounces frozen, cooked king crab** and **1 large, ripe avocado, diced,** for shrimp.

Creamy Shrimp Curry: Substitute desired amount of **Creamy Curry Sauce (see page 86)** for cream cheese, peanut butter, and curry.

Haddock Pudding Foldovers

1 pound frozen haddock,
  partially thawed
1 cup Rich Sauce for Fish (see
  page 89)
4 warm dinner crepes
  Paprika

1. Place fish in a greased baking dish.
2. Bake at 375°F 15 minutes. Remove from dish and flake.
3. Combine fish with ½ cup warm sauce. Spoon fish mixture on half of a crepe; fold over. Top each crepe with 2 tablespoons sauce, sprinkle with paprika, and serve immediately.

4 filled crepes

Note: Sole, flounder, or turbot may be substituted for haddock.

Herbed Scallop Turnovers

4 tablespoons butter or margarine
1 pound frozen scallops
2 tablespoons flour
1 clove garlic, crushed
2 teaspoons lemon juice
2 teaspoons lime juice
¼ teaspoon seasoned salt
2 dashes Tabasco
1½ teaspoons parsley
⅛ teaspoon marjoram
1 scallion, minced
¼ cup light cream or half-and-half
Salt and pepper to taste
4 dinner crepes

1. In 1 tablespoon butter, sauté scallops until they turn white. Drain scallops, reserving ½ cup liquid.
2. Melt remaining butter; stir in flour. Cook for 1 minute.
3. Add garlic, lemon juice, lime juice, seasoned salt, Tabasco, parsley, marjoram, and scallion to flour mixture. Blend well. Cook until thick and glossy.
4. Remove from heat. Blend reserved liquid and cream into sauce. Return to heat; cook, stirring constantly, until smooth and thick.
5. Add scallops and season with salt and pepper. Assemble, using turnover method. Place on a baking sheet.
6. Bake at 375°F 10 minutes.

4 turnovers

Scallops and Broccoli au Gratin

2 tablespoons butter or margarine
5 ounces frozen chopped broccoli
1 scallion, chopped
1 pound frozen scallops
2 tablespoons white wine
1½ teaspoons lemon juice
2 dashes cayenne pepper
1 sprig parsley, chopped
⅓ cup shredded Swiss cheese
2 tablespoons grated Parmesan cheese
Salt and pepper
8 dinner crepes
½ cup Basic White Sauce (see page 84)
Nutmeg

1. Melt butter. Sauté broccoli and scallion in butter until broccoli is cooked.
2. Stir in scallops, wine, lemon juice, cayenne, and parsley. Simmer until scallops are tender.
3. Drain off liquid. Stir in cheeses. Salt and pepper to taste.
4. Assemble, using square turnover method. Place on baking sheet.
5. Bake at 375°F 10 minutes. Spoon 1 tablespoon white sauce over each square, sprinkle with nutmeg, and serve.

8 squares

Note: Crab or shrimp may be substituted for scallops.

Scallops and Mushrooms au Gratin

1 pound frozen bay scallops
Juice of 1 lime (about ¼ cup)
½ cup white wine
½ cup water
¼ teaspoon salt
⅛ teaspoon pepper

1. Sprinkle scallops with lime juice and place in a saucepan. Add wine, ½ cup water, ¼ teaspoon salt, ⅛ teaspoon pepper, and bay leaf. Bring to boiling over medium heat. Remove from heat and drain.
2. Sauté mushrooms in 1 tablespoon butter about 3 minutes.
3. Melt the remaining butter in a saucepan. Blend in flour.

½ medium bay leaf
½ pound mushrooms, cleaned and
    coarsely chopped
5 tablespoons butter or margarine
5 tablespoons flour
½ cup whipping cream*
½ cup water
¼ teaspoon salt
2 dashes pepper
¼ teaspoon dry mustard
    Dash cayenne pepper
¼ pound Swiss cheese, shredded
4 dinner crepes
    Paprika

Gradually add remaining liquids to the flour and butter. Stir in mushrooms. Continue cooking over medium heat, stirring constantly until sauce comes to boiling. Blend in remaining seasonings and cheese. Cook and stir until cheese melts

4. Reserve ½ cup sauce for topping. Fold scallops into remaining sauce. Divide filling among crepes. Fold in half, put into a baking dish, top with ½ cup sauce, and sprinkle with paprika.

5. Bake at 375°F 15 minutes. Serve on a warm plate. One filled crepe per person is an ample portion for a luncheon or light supper.

4 filled crepes

*If desired, substitute 1 cup milk for ½ cup cream and ½ cup water.

Walter's Clam Cannelloni

⅔ cup olive oil
2 large onions, chopped
1 medium green pepper, seeded
    and chopped
1 package (10 ounces) frozen
    chopped spinach, thawed
4 cans (10 ounces each) whole baby
    clams
    Salt and pepper
18 dinner crepes

1. Heat oil and sauté onion. Add green pepper and spinach; stir until ingredients are blended.
2. Drain clam juice into spinach mixture. Chop clams. Add to spinach mixture; season to taste with salt and pepper. Simmer, uncovered, 1½ hours. Mixture should be moist but not liquid. Spoon mixture down the center of the crepe. Fold in thirds. Put into a large baking dish. Drizzle any remaining juice over top.
3. Bake, covered, at 350°F 10 minutes. Serve 3 or 4 cannelloni per person.

18 filled crepes

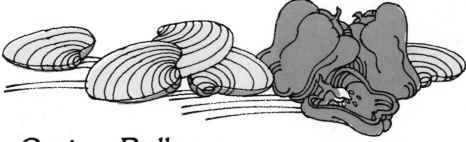

Clam Casino Rolls

1 can (10 ounces) whole baby clams
3 slices bacon, diced
2 scallions, sliced
3 tablespoons chopped green
    pepper
1 teaspoon minced fresh parsley
2 tablespoons flour
1 teaspoon lemon juice
    Salt and pepper

1. Drain clams; reserve broth. Coarsely chop clams and set aside.
2. Sauté bacon, scallions, green pepper, and parsley until tender, but not browned. Remove from heat; stir in flour, ¾ cup reserved clam broth (water may be added to make ¾ cup), and lemon juice. Return to heat; cook, stirring constantly, until thickened.
3. Stir clams into sauce; season to taste. Spread a thin layer of sauce over crepe; assemble, using jelly-roll method. Put into a baking dish.
4. Bake at 375°F 15 minutes.

6 rolls

Note: Each roll may be cut in bite-size pieces and served on wooden picks as hors d'oeuvres. Makes about 36 pieces.

Sole Royale

2 pounds fillet of sole
2 slices onion
  Celery tops
  Water to cover
1 package (10 ounces) frozen
    chopped spinach
¼ cup minced onion
¼ cup butter or margarine
1⅓ cups Mushroom-Garlic Spread
    (see page 21)
8 dinner crepes
2 cups Rich Cheese Sauce (see
    page 85)

1. Place fish, onion, and celery tops in a skillet. Cover with water. Simmer gently until fish is tender, but not flaky. Fish should be firm and white in color.
2. Cook spinach following directions on package. Drain well.
3. Sauté onion in butter until cooked but not browned. Add mushroom spread and spinach; simmer 1 minute, stirring constantly.
4. Spread mixture over crepes. Gently place whole pieces of fish on half of each crepe. Fold in half. Put on a baking sheet. Top each turnover with ¼ cup cheese sauce.
5. Bake at 375°F 15 minutes.

8 filled crepes

Oysters Goldenrod in Turnovers

4 hard-cooked eggs
1 pint fresh oysters or 1 can
    (8 ounces) oysters
6 slices bacon, chopped
¼ cup flour
  Oyster liquid plus enough milk
    to equal 1 cup
  Salt and pepper
8 dinner crepes

1. Separate egg yolks and whites. Chop whites and grate yolks; set aside.
2. Place oysters in saucepan with their liquid. Simmer until edges curl. Drain, reserve liquid. Cut oysters in half and set aside.
3. Sauté bacon, reserve drippings. Make a white sauce with 1 tablespoon bacon fat, flour, oyster liquid, and milk. Stir chopped egg whites and bacon into sauce.
4. Combine the sauce and oysters while sauce is still hot. Salt and pepper to taste. Assemble, using turnover method. Place on baking sheet.
5. Bake at 375°F 10 minutes. Remove from oven; place on serving dish. Brush crepes with remaining sauce, top with grated egg yolk, and serve immediately.

8 turnovers

Mussels Sicilian Style

4 tablespoons butter or margarine
½ cup chopped onion
4 scallions, chopped
1 large clove garlic, minced
1 can (16 ounces) whole tomatoes,
    drained and broken

1. Melt butter in skillet. Stir in onion, scallions, garlic, tomatoes, parsley, thyme, marjoram, and bay leaf. Cook until simmering; add wine.
2. Add fresh mussels (if using canned mussels, see Note), cover skillet, and simmer until shells open. Remove shells. Cut mussels in half and return to sauce.

2 tablespoons chopped fresh
    parsley
½ teaspoon thyme
¼ teaspoon marjoram
½ bay leaf
½ cup dry white wine
2 dozen mussels, cleaned, or
    1 can (8 ounces) mussels
4 dinner crepes

3. Assemble, using egg-roll method. Place in a baking pan, seam side down. Top with remaining sauce.
4. Bake at 375°F 10 minutes.

4 filled crepes

Note: When using canned mussels, omit step 2. Instead, simmer sauce until onion is clear, add mussels, and cook 3 minutes.

Tuna Bake

2 tablespoons oil
¼ cup chopped onion
1 package (10 ounces) frozen
    chopped broccoli
1 can (13 ounces) tuna, drained
    and flaked
1 cup Quick Creamy Fish Sauce
    (see page 87)
8 dinner crepes

1. Heat oil; sauté onion and broccoli. When broccoli is tender, stir in tuna. Remove from heat; stir in ½ cup of Quick Creamy Fish Sauce.
2. Assemble, using square turnover method. Arrange in baking dish; cover with remaining sauce.
3. Bake at 375°F 20 minutes. Serve immediately.

8 squares

Note: ¾ pound cooked cod or flounder may be substituted for the tuna.

Tuna Quickie

1 can (13 ounces) tuna, drained
¼ cup mayonnaise
1 teaspoon lemon juice
6 dinner crepes
½ cup Hollandaise Verde (see page
    84)

1. Flake tuna. Combine tuna, mayonnaise, and lemon juice. Spread tuna mixture on crepes. Roll up, using jelly-roll method, and place on a baking sheet.
2. Bake at 350°F 15 minutes. Top with Hollandaise Verde, and serve.

6 rolls

Salmon Pacifica

1 can (16 ounces) salmon
¼ cup chopped green onion
½ pound fresh mushrooms, chopped
½ cup plus 2 tablespoons butter
5 tablespoons flour
2 cups milk
1 cup whipping cream
¾ teaspoon salt
    Dash cayenne pepper
1½ cups shredded Swiss cheese
10 to 12 dinner crepes
¼ cup grated Parmesan cheese

1. Drain and flake salmon, reserving liquid. Sauté onion and mushrooms in ¼ cup butter. Stir in salmon and reserved liquid.
2. Melt remaining 6 tablespoons butter in a saucepan and blend in flour. Gradually stir in milk and whipping cream. Cook, stirring constantly, until thickened and smooth. Stir in salt and pepper.
3. Add about ¾ cup cream sauce to the salmon mixture. Stir gently and set aside. Blend Swiss cheese into remaining cream sauce and heat until cheese melts.
4. Spoon a thin layer of cheese sauce into bottom of a buttered baking dish. Assemble crepes, using tube method, and arrange over sauce. Spoon remaining sauce over crepes. Sprinkle with Parmesan cheese.
5. Bake at 375°F 30 minutes, or until golden brown and bubbly.

10 to 12 filled crepes

Salmon Turnovers

1 can (7¾ ounces) salmon
¼ cup mayonnaise
2 tablespoons sweet relish, drained
1 teaspoon grated onion
1 hard-cooked egg, finely diced or
    shredded
¼ teaspoon salt
    Dash freshly ground pepper
4 dinner crepes

1. Drain and flake salmon. Stir in mayonnaise, sweet relish, onion, egg, salt, and pepper. Blend well. Assemble, using turnover method.
2. Bake at 375°F 10 minutes. Serve immediately with a **green vegetable.**

4 turnovers

Creamy Salmon

1 can (7¾ ounces) salmon
⅓ cup minced celery
2 tablespoons chopped sweet pickle
¼ teaspoon salt
1 cup Creamy Lemon Sauce (see
    page 89)
4 dinner crepes

1. Drain and flake salmon. Stir in celery, pickle, and salt. Add just enough Creamy Lemon Sauce (about ¼ cup) to moisten salmon mixture.
2. Assemble, using tube method. Place on baking sheet, seam side down.
3. Bake at 350°F 15 minutes. Top with remaining sauce and serve.

4 filled crepes

Note: Tuna may be substituted for salmon.

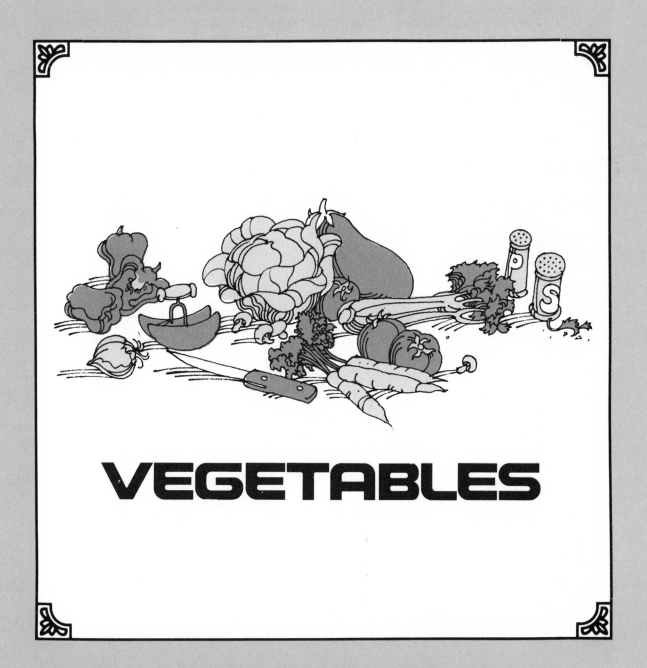

VEGETABLES

Asparagus Supreme

3 tablespoons softened butter or
   margarine
3 teaspoons prepared mustard
6 dinner crepes
6 slices (1 ounce each) cooked
   ham
18 cooked asparagus spears
6 slices Swiss cheese, cut
   diagonally in half
6 slices American cheese, cut
   diagonally in half

1. Cream butter with mustard. Spread butter mixture on crepes. Cover with a slice of ham. Place 3 asparagus spears in center of each crepe. Fold in thirds. Put on a baking sheet. Arrange 2 triangles of each cheese alternately over each crepe.
2. Broil until cheese begins to melt. Serve immediately.

6 filled crepes

Hot Bean and Bacon Turnovers

4 slices bacon
2 tablespoons flour
½ cup milk
2 tablespoons distilled vinegar
4 teaspoons sugar
   Salt and pepper
1 can (16 ounces) french style
   green beans, drained
1 hard-cooked egg, diced
4 dinner crepes

1. Dice 2 slices bacon and fry until crisp. Stir in flour. Add milk gradually, stirring constantly. Cook until thick. Add vinegar and sugar. Season with salt and pepper to taste.
2. Combine green beans and diced egg. Pour sauce over beans and egg. Toss until well blended.
3. Assemble, using turnover method.
4. Bake at 375°F 10 minutes.
5. Meanwhile, cut remaining bacon slices in half. Fry until crisp.
6. Serve turnovers hot garnished with bacon.

4 turnovers

Broccoli Foldovers

1 recipe Mushroom Cheese Spread
   (see Pinwheel Party Platter,
   page 16)
3 cups chopped cooked broccoli
9 dinner crepes
   Paprika

1. Prepare spread. Reserve one third of spread for topping.
2. Combine the remaining spread with broccoli. Divide broccoli mixture among crepes. Fold in half. Put on a baking sheet. Top with reserved spread. Sprinkle with paprika.
3. Bake at 375°F 10 minutes. Serve on warm plates.

9 filled crepes

Note: For variation, substitute chopped cauliflower or cut green beans for broccoli. A slice of ham or turkey can be put on crepe before adding filling.

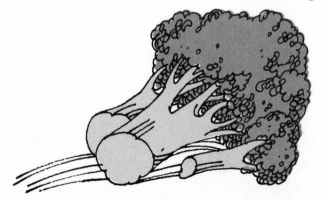

Eggplant Cordon Bleu

¼ cup oil
1 eggplant (1 pound), pared and diced
½ cup minced celery
½ cup chopped onion
1 teaspoon salt
¼ teaspoon fresh black pepper
½ cup water
⅓ cup chopped boiled ham
⅓ cup shredded Swiss cheese
½ teaspoon oregano
8 dinner crepes

1. Heat oil and sauté eggplant, celery, and onion. Season with salt and pepper. Add water and simmer 5 minutes. Stir in ham, cheese, and oregano.
2. Assemble, using tube method. Place the tube, fold side down, on a baking sheet.
3. Bake at 375°F 20 minutes. Serve hot.

8 filled crepes

Eggplant Parmesan

1 medium eggplant (about 1 pound)
½ cup oil
1 medium clove garlic, crushed in a garlic press
1 teaspoon oregano
1 cup tomato sauce
¼ cup grated Parmesan cheese
¼ pound mozzarella cheese
8 dinner crepes

1. Pare and dice eggplant. Sauté in oil until tender (about 7 to 10 minutes). Stir in garlic and oregano; continue cooking 3 to 5 minutes. Remove from heat. Drain off any liquid. Stir in ½ cup tomato sauce; simmer 5 minutes. Remove from heat. Add grated cheese.
2. Shred half of the mozzarella and add to eggplant mixture.
3. Assemble, using square turnover method. Place on a baking sheet. Top with slices of remaining mozzarella cheese.
4. Bake at 375°F 15 minutes. Serve topped with remaining sauce.

8 filled crepes

Mushroom Stack

1 pound mushrooms, cleaned and finely chopped
2 tablespoons butter
1 cup Creamy Brown Sauce (see page 89)
8 dinner crepes
   Parsley for garnish

1. Sauté mushrooms in butter until mushrooms are cooked and pan is almost dry. Stir in sauce.
2. Assemble by stacking 1 crepe, mushroom filling, crepe, mushroom filling, crepe, filling, crepe; form 2 stacks. Put on a baking sheet.
3. Bake at 375°F 10 minutes.
4. Cut into wedges and serve for brunch or as an appetizer. Garnish with parsley.

8 servings

Mushroom-Chicken Stack: Follow recipe for Mushroom Stack. Spread contents of a **4½-ounce can chicken spread** on 2 crepes. Stack crepe, mushroom filling, crepe with chicken, crepe, mushroom, crepe. If desired, mix **1 cup Basic White Sauce** (see page 84) and **1 cup cooked chopped spinach;** spread on each stack before serving.

Mushroom and Bean Bake

2 tablespoons butter or margarine
1 can (2 ounces) sliced
    mushrooms, drained
¼ cup chopped onion
2 tablespoons flour
½ cup milk
¼ teaspoon thyme
    Salt and pepper
1 can (16 ounces) french style
    green beans, drained
6 dinner crepes

1. Melt butter. Sauté mushrooms and onion until tender but not brown. Stir in flour. Gradually add milk, stirring constantly. Cook until thick. Stir in thyme. Season to taste with salt and pepper. Stir in beans.
2. Assemble, using tube method. Place on a baking sheet seam side down.
3. Bake at 375°F 10 minutes.

6 filled crepes

Curried Potato Logs

3 medium potatoes*
1 egg, slightly beaten
¾ cup Curried Cheese Sauce
    (see page 85)
½ teaspoon salt
9 crepes
    Butter or margarine

1. Pare and cook potatoes in lightly salted water. Mash. Yield should be approximately 2½ cups.
2. Beat egg into mashed potatoes. Add sauce and salt; blend well. Divide potato mixture among crepes. Assemble, using egg-roll method. Fry in butter in a skillet until golden brown on all sides. Serve hot.

9 potato logs

*If desired, substitute 2½ cups instant mashed potatoes for freshly mashed potatoes.

Spinach-Bacon Turnovers

4 slices bacon, diced
⅓ cup chopped onion
1 package (10 ounces) frozen
    chopped spinach, thawed
¼ cup mayonnaise
    Salt and pepper
4 dinner crepes
1 cup Basic White Sauce (see
    page 84) and 1 tablespoon
    bacon bits (optional)

1. Sauté bacon and onion until bacon is cooked.
2. Drain spinach well. Stir-fry spinach with bacon and onion for 3 minutes. Drain mixture well. Stir in mayonnaise and season with salt and pepper to taste.
3. Assemble, using turnover method. Place on a baking sheet.
4. Bake at 375°F 10 minutes. If desired, serve topped with white sauce and sprinkled with bacon bits.

4 turnovers

Spinach Florentine

2 pounds fresh spinach
6 tablespoons butter or
   margarine
1 medium onion, chopped
6 tablespoons flour
1 cup milk
1 teaspoon salt
¼ pound Swiss cheese, coarsely
   shredded
¼ teaspoon Tabasco
½ pound mushrooms, cleaned and
   coarsely chopped
8 dinner crepes
¼ cup whipping cream, whipped

1. Clean spinach. Steam spinach in covered saucepot for 4 minutes. Drain thoroughly and coarsely chop. Set aside.
2. Melt 4 tablespoons butter. Sauté onion about 10 minutes. Stir in flour. Continue stirring and cook 1 minute. Gradually add milk, stirring constantly. Stir and cook until mixture boils; boil 1 minute. Remove from heat. Stir in salt, Tabasco, and cheese. Reserve ½ cup sauce for topping.
3. Sauté mushrooms in 2 tablespoons butter. Add mushrooms and spinach to sauce for filling. Divide filling among crepes and fold in half. Put into a baking dish. (Crepes can be refrigerated at this point, but bring them to room temperature before baking.)
4. Bake at 350°F 30 minutes. Fold whipped cream into reserved sauce. Spoon over baked crepes and broil until sauce bubbles.

8 filled crepes

Note: If desired, place a slice of ham on each crepe before filling.

Spinach Roll

1 package (10 ounces) frozen
   chopped spinach
2 tablespoons butter or margarine
1 medium onion, coarsely chopped
⅔ cup Mushroom-Garlic Spread
   (see page 21)
6 dinner crepes
½ cup Lemon Sauce (see page 88)

1. Place frozen spinach, butter, and onion in a saucepan. Cover. Cook until spinach is thawed. Remove cover, cook, stirring occasionally, until liquid evaporates. Blend in mushroom spread. Cook 5 minutes, stirring constantly.
2. Divide spinach filling among crepes. Assemble, using tube method. Spread sauce over filled crepes.
3. Bake at 375°F 10 minutes. Serve hot.

6 filled crepes

Stuffed Squash Logs

1¼ cups mashed squash (butternut,
    Hubbard, acorn)
1 tablespoon butter or margarine
1 tablespoon maple syrup
10 dinner crepes
10 cooked breakfast sausages
    (8-ounce package)

1. Combine mashed squash, butter, and maple syrup.
2. Spread about 2 tablespoons of squash mixture on each crepe. Place 1 sausage on each crepe and assemble, using egg-roll method. Place seam side down on a baking sheet.
3. Bake at 375°F 15 minutes.

10 logs

Note: Mashed sweet potatoes or mashed carrots may be substituted for squash. Turkey can be substituted for sausage and logs can be topped with warmed cranberry sauce.

Tomato Rabbit

4 slices bacon, diced
2 tablespoons flour
½ cup shredded Cheddar cheese
2 tablespoons sherry
  Dash cayenne pepper
2 medium tomatoes
4 dinner crepes

1. Cook bacon until crisp. Remove bacon and drain; reserve bacon drippings.
2. To 2 tablespoons of bacon drippings add flour, ¼ cup cheese, sherry, and cayenne. Stir until well blended. Cook over medium heat until thick; cool.
3. Core tomatoes and dice. Mix tomato and cooked bacon pieces with sauce.
4. Divide sauce among crepes, fold in half, top with remaining cheese, and serve.

4 filled crepes

Zucchini Italiano

1 pound zucchini, diced
1 large clove garlic, crushed in a
  garlic press
1 can (16 ounces) tomatoes,
  drained and diced
½ cup chopped onion
  Salt and pepper
¼ cup grated Parmesan cheese
8 dinner crepes

1. Combine diced zucchini, garlic, tomatoes, onion, salt, and pepper in a saucepan. Simmer 25 to 30 minutes over medium heat, or until squash is tender.
2. Place crepes on a baking sheet. Drain zucchini mixture as you spoon it equally onto each crepe. Sprinkle with 2 tablespoons cheese. Fold crepes in half, brush with juice from cooked squash, and sprinkle with remaining 2 tablespoons cheese.
3. Bake at 375°F 15 minutes. Serve immediately while crisp and hot.

8 filled crepes

Note: Serve without baking, if desired.

Zucchini with Pesto Sauce

1 pound zucchini
  Water
3 tablespoons grated onion
½ teaspoon salt
¼ teaspoon pepper
⅔ cup Pesto Sauce (see page 88)
8 dinner crepes

1. Wash, remove stems, and dice zucchini. Place in a saucepan and cover with water. Stir in onion, salt, and pepper. Simmer 7 to 10 minutes, or until squash is tender. Drain well. Toss with Pesto Sauce. Spoon onto crepes and fold in half. Put into a baking dish.
2. Bake at 375°F 10 minutes. Serve immediately.

8 filled crepes

Oriental Vegetable Rolls

¼ cup oil
2 tablespoons soy sauce
2 cups fresh bean sprouts or 1 cup
  canned bean sprouts
½ pound mushrooms, cleaned
  and sliced

1. Heat oil and soy sauce. When hot, sauté bean sprouts, mushrooms, scallions, bok choy, and water chestnuts. Season with salt and pepper to taste.
2. Assemble, using egg-roll method; drain vegetables with a slotted spoon.
3. Melt butter, pan-fry vegetable rolls by placing them in hot

4 scallions, chopped
2 cups chopped bok choy (Chinese green cabbage)
6 water chestnuts, minced
 Salt and pepper
12 dinner crepes
¼ cup butter or margarine

butter seam side down until browned, and then turning them over to brown the top.
4. Serve immediately. Top with bottled sweet-and-sour duck sauce, if desired.

12 rolls

Vegetables Creole

4 slices bacon, diced
1 package (10 ounces) frozen french style green beans
1 package (10 ounces) frozen succotash
1 can (8 ounces) tomatoes
1 teaspoon dried minced onion
1 beef bouillon cube
2 tablespoons Chili Sauce (see page 87)
2 tablespoons flour
8 dinner crepes

1. Sauté bacon until crisp. Drain and reserve drippings. Add beans, succotash, tomatoes, onion, bouillon cube, and Chili Sauce to bacon pieces. Stir and cook until heated.
2. Stir flour into reserved bacon drippings. Stir into vegetable mixture. Simmer, stirring occasionally, until thick.
3. Assemble, using square turnover method; drain vegetables with a slotted spoon. Place filled crepes, seam side down, on a baking sheet.
4. Bake at 375°F 10 minutes. Serve topped with remaining warmed sauce.

8 filled crepes

Vegetable Medley

3 tablespoons butter or margarine
1 package (10 ounces) frozen chopped broccoli
3 tablespoons grated carrot
2 scallions, minced
2 tablespoons minced celery
1 can (2 ounces) mushrooms, drained
⅛ teaspoon garlic powder
 Salt and pepper
¾ cup Lima Bean Spread (see page 22)
8 dinner crepes
¼ cup grated Parmesan cheese
 Paprika

1. Melt butter. Sauté broccoli, carrot, scallions, celery, and mushrooms until tender. Remove from heat and drain. Stir in garlic powder and season with salt and pepper to taste. Stir in bean spread.
2. Assemble, using square turnover method. Place on a baking sheet; sprinkle with cheese and paprika.
3. Bake at 375°F 10 minutes. Serve immediately.

8 filled crepes

Creamy Vegetable Squares

2 tablespoons butter or margarine
2 tablespoons minced scallion
2 tablespoons grated carrot
¼ pound mushrooms, cleaned and sliced
1 package (10 ounces) frozen chopped spinach, thawed and well drained
1 pound cottage cheese
1 egg, slightly beaten
½ teaspoon Italian seasoning
¼ teaspoon ground thyme
¼ cup grated Parmesan cheese
12 dinner crepes

1. Melt butter. Sauté scallion, carrot, mushrooms, and spinach until all are tender. Drain well. Cool.
2. Beat cottage cheese and egg until well blended. Add Italian seasoning, thyme, and 2 tablespoons of grated cheese.
3. Assemble, using square turnover method. Place on a baking sheet, seam side down. Sprinkle with remaining cheese.
4. Bake at 350°F 20 minutes. Cool 5 minutes before serving.

12 filled crepes

Vegetables au Gratin

2 tablespoons butter or margarine
⅓ cup chopped Bermuda onion
½ cup chopped green pepper
¼ cup sliced ripe olives
½ cup chopped mushrooms
6 dinner crepes
½ cup shredded Cheddar cheese
¼ cup Chili Sauce (see page 87)
½ cup dairy sour cream

1. Melt butter. Sauté onion, pepper, olives, and mushrooms until cooked.
2. Spread mixture on crepes; sprinkle with cheese. Roll up jelly-roll fashion. Place in a baking dish; top with sauce made by combining Chili Sauce and sour cream.
3. Bake at 350°F 10 minutes. Serve hot.

6 filled crepes

CHEESE AND EGGS

Egg-and-Nut-Filled Crepes

¾ teaspoon salt
½ teaspoon ground coriander
⅛ teaspoon white pepper
    Few grains paprika
6 tablespoons mayonnaise
3 hard-cooked eggs, chopped
½ cup filberts, finely chopped
½ cup diced celery
10 dinner crepes
2 cups Cheddar Cheese Sauce (see page 85)

1. Combine salt, coriander, pepper, and paprika; blend with mayonnaise. Mix in the eggs, filberts, and celery.
2. Assemble crepes, using tube method. Place crepes in a shallow baking dish. Cover with the Cheddar Cheese Sauce.
3. Bake at 375°F about 20 minutes, or until sauce is bubbly.

10 filled crepes

Sweet Cheese Blintzes

1 pound cottage cheese
1 egg
2 teaspoons sugar
½ teaspoon salt
8 saltines, crushed
12 dinner crepes
3 to 4 tablespoons butter or margarine

1. Press cottage cheese through a sieve. Beat in egg until mixture is light. Blend in sugar and salt. Stir in saltines, blending thoroughly.
2. Assemble, using egg-roll method, brown side of crepe inside.
3. Heat butter in a large skillet until foamy. Place blintzes in butter, seam side down. Cook on each side until golden brown (3 to 5 minutes). Blot.
4. Serve hot with **jelly or dairy sour cream**, or sprinkle with **cinnamon and sugar**.

12 blintzes

Manicotti

1 pound cottage cheese
2 eggs, beaten
2 tablespoons grated Parmesan cheese
2 teaspoons oregano
1 clove garlic, crushed in a garlic press; or use ½ teaspoon garlic powder
    Salt and pepper
6 dinner crepes
1 cup marinara sauce*
¼ pound mozzarella cheese, thinly sliced

1. Press cottage cheese through a sieve. Combine with eggs, grated cheese, oregano, and garlic. Add salt and pepper to taste. Beat until fluffy.
2. Divide filling among 6 crepes. Roll, using tube method. Place close together in baking dish; top with sauce and mozzarella cheese.
3. Bake at 375°F 30 minutes. Serve piping hot.

6 filled crepes

*Meat sauce can be used.

Lasagne Tarts

1 pound ricotta cheese
1 egg, beaten
½ medium clove garlic, crushed in a garlic press
½ teaspoon oregano

1. Combine ricotta cheese, egg, garlic, oregano, ¼ cup mozzarella and ¼ cup Parmesan cheese. Set aside.
2. Combine remaining mozzarella and ¼ cup Parmesan.
3. Assemble, using tart method; use a rounded tablespoonful of ricotta mixture, 2 slices sausage, a sprinkle of mozza-

¾ cup shredded mozzarella cheese
⅔ cup grated Parmesan cheese
8 dinner crepes
¾ pound Italian sausage, cooked
   and sliced
½ cup bottled spaghetti sauce

rella-Parmesan cheese mixture, and 1 teaspoon sauce in layers; ease crepe into muffin cup and repeat layering except for sauce.
4. Bake at 375°F 10 minutes; turn oven control to 325°F and continue baking 30 minutes. Cool 10 minutes.
5. Warm remaining sauce. Remove tarts form muffin cup. Serve topped with remaining sauce and grated cheese.

8 tarts

Crepes Benedict

12 eggs
   Salt and pepper
2 tablespoons butter or
   margarine
8 thin slices boiled ham, heated
8 dinner crepes
1 cup hollandaise (see page 84)

1. Beat eggs with salt and pepper to taste.
2. Melt butter. Soft-scramble eggs in butter.
3. To assemble, put 1 slice of ham on each crepe and spoon eggs on top. Fold crepe and ham over eggs and serve topped with warm hollandaise.

8 filled crepes

Quiche Tarts

4 slices bacon, diced
¼ cup chopped onion
⅛ teaspoon cayenne pepper
4 eggs, beaten
8 ounces dairy sour cream
¼ teaspoon nutmeg
8 dinner crepes
   Nutmeg

1. Sauté bacon, onion, and cayenne until onion is soft. Cool.
2. Combine eggs, sour cream, and ¼ teaspoon nutmeg; stir until well blended.
3. Assemble, using tart method; use bacon-onion mixture as the filling, fitting the crepe down into the muffin cup and topping with sour cream-egg mixture. Sprinkle with nutmeg.
4. Bake at 375°F 10 minutes. Turn oven control to 325°F and continue baking 30 minutes.
5. Cool 5 minutes. Remove from cups and serve warm.

8 tarts

Mexican Quiche Tarts: Follow recipe for Quiche Tarts; add ⅓ **cup drained canned Mexican corn** (corn with peppers) to filling.

Tongue Quiche Tarts: Follow recipe for Quiche Tarts; substitute **cooked diced tongue** for bacon and add **½ cup drained cooked spinach** to egg mixture. This will make filling for 10 tarts.

Ham Quiche Tarts: Follow recipe for Quiche Tarts; substitute ⅓ **cup chopped cooked ham** sautéed in **2 teaspoons butter** for bacon.

Mushroom Quiche Tarts: Follow recipe for Quiche Tarts; substitute ⅓ **cup chopped mushrooms,** sautéed in **1 tablespoon butter** for bacon.

Crab Quiche Tarts: Follow recipe for Quiche Tarts; substiture ⅓ **cup flaked crab meat** and **1 tablespoon chopped ripe olives,** sautéed in **1 tablespoon butter,** for onion and bacon.

Pears and Cheddar

3 large firm pears, pared,
  cored, and cut in eighths*
  Boiling water to cover
½ pound extra-sharp aged Cheddar
  cheese, coarsely shredded
6 hot crepes

1. Place pears in boiling water. Simmer gently 15 minutes, or until tender. Drain.
2. Combine ½ cup loosely packed cheese with hot pears.
3. Place 4 pear wedges on each crepe and fold. Sprinkle remaining cheese over crepes. Serve immediately.

6 filled crepes

Note: If desired, top with Cheddar Cheese Sauce (see page 85) and sprinkle with shredded cheese.

*Canned pears can be substituted for fresh pears.

Crepes for Breakfast

10 eggs
  Salt and pepper
2 tablespoons butter or margarine
8 dinner crepes

1. Beat eggs with salt and pepper to taste.
2. Melt butter. Soft-scramble eggs in butter.
3. To assemble, spoon eggs on half of each crepe. Use any of the following suggestions; fold and serve.

8 filled crepes

Suggestions:
1. Add **1 teaspoon sugar** to eggs; top folded crepe with **Strawberry Sauce** (see page 91).
2. Sauté **¼ pound sliced mushrooms** in a small amount of butter. Spoon onto eggs.
3. Slice **cooked breakfast sausage** (a 10-ounce package) and put on eggs; top crepes with **Apple Sauce.** (see page 90).
4. Sauté **⅓ cup minced onion** and **2 ounces lox** in a small amount of **butter.** Spoon onto eggs.
5. Put a **breakfast sausage** in each crepe with eggs; top crepes with **warm applesauce or Spanish Sauce** (see page 86).
6. Dot eggs with **jam** or **jelly;** sprinkle top with **confectioners' sugar.**
7. Spread **¾ cup Béarnaise Sauce** (see page 84) over eggs.
8. Crumble **8 slices crisp bacon** over eggs.

Blintzes

2 scallions, minced
¼ cup butter or margarine
1 teaspoon chopped parsley
1 pound pot cheese or cottage
  cheese

1. Sauté scallions in 1 tablespoon butter. Stir in parsley. Drain off liquid. Set aside.
2. Beat cheese with egg yolk until smooth. Add bread crumbs, scallions with parsley, and salt and pepper to taste.
3. Assemble, using egg-roll method, brown side of crepe inside.

1 egg, separated
3 tablespoons bread crumbs
  Salt and pepper
12 dinner crepes
8 ounces dairy sour cream
  Caviar (optional)

Brush outer edge of crepe with egg white to seal. Place on flat plate or in a shallow pan; cover and chill 1 hour. Remove from refrigerator.
4. Heat remaining butter until foamy. Place blintz in butter, seam side down. Watching carefully, cook on each side until golden brown (3 to 5 minutes). Blot.
5. Serve topped with sour cream. For extra elegance, dot sour cream with caviar.

12 blintzes

Crepes Rustica

1 pound ricotta cheese
1 egg, beaten
½ pound mozzarella cheese, shredded
¼ cup grated Parmesan cheese
¼ teaspoon oregano
1 pound Italian sausage, cooked and crumbled
18 dinner crepes
2 cups Parmesan Sauce (see page 84)
2 teaspoons dry mustard
½ teaspoon nutmeg
6 slices salami, cut in strips

1. Combine ricotta, egg, ½ cup mozzarella cheese, grated Parmesan cheese, and oregano. Reserve for filling.
2. Assemble, using square turnover method, layering sausage, remaining mozzarella cheese, and ricotta mixture; fold. Put on a baking sheet.
3. Make cheese sauce; stir in mustard and nutmeg. Put a spoonful of sauce on top and crisscross 2 strips of salami.
4. Bake at 375°F 20 minutes. Cool 10 minutes. Serve 2 for dinner and 1 for appetizer.

18 filled crepes

Curried Eggs

8 hard-cooked eggs
1½ cups Curry Sauce (see page 84)
⅓ cup minced onion
1 tablespoon butter or margarine
1 chicken bouillon cube
2 tablespoons ketchup
1 cup cooked peas (canned or frozen)
8 dinner crepes
  Paprika

1. Dice eggs. Stir eggs into sauce.
2. Sauté onion in butter; add bouillon cube and ketchup. Stir and cook until bouillon is dissolved. Blend mixture into eggs and sauce. Heat until bubbling. Stir in peas.
3. To assemble, put filling on half of crepe, fold over, and top with some sauce and paprika.
4. Serve warm with your favorite curry condiments (see page 40).

8 filled crepes

Bacon and Egg Foldovers au Gratin

4 slices bacon
3 large eggs, beaten
1 tablespoon milk
2 dinner crepes
1 ounce Cheddar cheese, thinly
    sliced

1. Cook bacon until crisp; drain.
2. Combine eggs and milk in the top of a double boiler. Stir while cooking over boiling water until eggs thicken. Mixture should be soft, but able to hold its shape when mounded; do not overcook.
3. Divide eggs in half; spoon into crepes. Top each with 2 bacon slices. Fold in half. Place cheese over crepe. Put onto a baking sheet.
4. Bake at 375°F 3 to 5 minutes, or until cheese melts. Serve immediately.

2 servings

Spanish Crepes

¼ cup chopped green pepper
2 scallions, chopped
2 ounces boiled ham, diced
8 eggs, beaten
6 dinner crepes
1 cup Spanish Sauce (see page 86)

1. Sauté green pepper, scallions, and ham until pepper is tender. Stir in beaten eggs. Cook until soft-scrambled.
2. Spoon egg mixture onto half of each crepe. Fold over and serve topped with hot sauce.

6 filled crepes

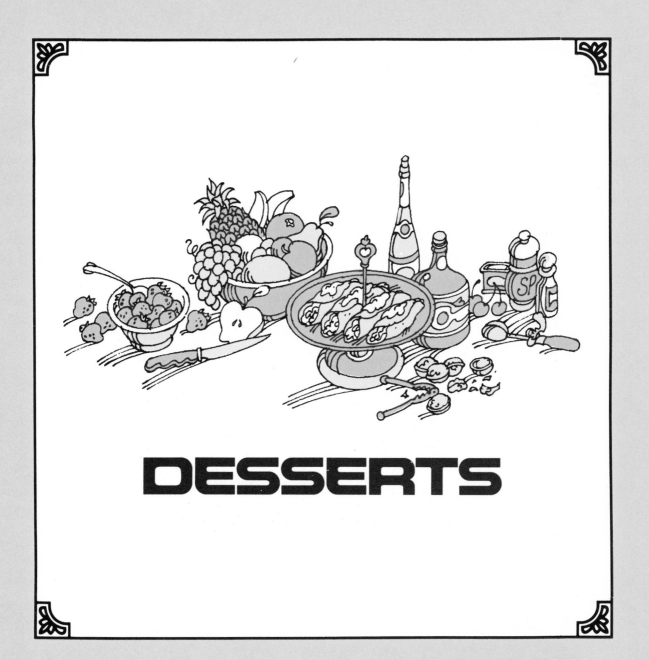

DESSERTS

Almond Bavarian Logs

1 envelope unflavored gelatin
1 cup milk
3 eggs, separated
    Dash salt
⅓ cup sugar
1 tablespoon almond liqueur
½ cup whipping cream, whipped
⅓ cup crushed macaroons
12 dessert crepes
¼ cup finely chopped toasted
    almonds

1. Sprinkle gelatin over ⅓ cup milk to soften.
2. Scald remaining milk over medium heat.
3. Beat egg yolks with salt and 2 tablespoons sugar. Gradually stir in scalded milk, then softened gelatin.
4. Cook mixture in the top of a double boiler over simmering water. Cook and stir until mixture coats a metal spoon (about 15 minutes).
5. Cool 10 minutes. Stir in liqueur. Chill by placing pan over a bowl of ice and water for 30 minutes, or until it mounds.
6. Beat egg whites until soft peaks form; gradually add remaining sugar and beat until stiff. Fold in whipped cream, pudding mixture, and macaroons.
7. Assemble, using tube method. Sprinkle ends with nuts.

12 logs

Ambrosia 'n' Crepes

1 pint strawberries, puréed in
    in blender
3 tablespoons kirsch
3 tablespoons Grand Marnier
1 tablespoon sugar
18 dessert crepes
1 pint strawberries, sliced
2 bananas, sliced
½ cup canned crushed pineapple,
    drained
1 quart vanilla ice cream
6 tablespoons flaked coconut

1. Combine puréed strawberries, kirsch, Grand Marnier, and sugar in a chafing dish; cook until bubbly. Add crepes according to hot sauce method.
2. When all crepes are coated with syrup and folded, ignite sauce. When flames die down, stir in sliced strawberries, bananas, and pineapple. Simmer 3 minutes.
3. To serve, arrange 3 crepes on a plate, top with ice cream and hot fruit. Sprinkle with coconut.

6 servings

Angel Crepes

1 package (6½ ounces)
    fluffy white frosting*
    Boiling water
6 dessert crepes

1. Prepare frosting with boiling water following package instructions.
2. Spread on crepes to ⅛ inch from edge. Put on a baking sheet.
3. Bake at 350°F 10 minutes.
4. Serve as a large cookie or stack with a filling such as **chocolate pudding** or **fruit**.

6 angel crepes

*This is a quick substitute for meringue.

Apple-Nut-Raisin Stack: Add **1 tablespoon raisins, 1 tablespoon chopped nuts,** and **2 tablespoons shredded apple** to frosting. Stack with **sliced cooked apples** for filling.

Date-Nut Stack: Add **2 tablespoons chopped dates** and

1 tablespoon chopped nuts. Stack with **canned prune filling.**

Cinnamon-Nut Stack: Add **3 tablespoons nuts** and **1 teaspoon cinnamon.** Stack with **apple or pumpkin filling.**

Chocolate Angel Crepes: Fold in **2 ounces grated semisweet chocolate.**

Apple Stack: Toss **1 cup cooked sliced apples,** still warm, with **¼ cup chunky peanut butter** and **¼ teaspoon cinnamon.** Stack with peanut butter-apple mixture as filling.

Apple-Nut Crisp

2 medium Granny Smith green apples (or any tart baking apple)
¼ teaspoon cinnamon
6 tablespoons packed brown sugar
¼ cup flour
2 tablespoons margarine
2 tablespoons chunky peanut butter
4 dessert crepes
1 pint ice cream (optional)

1. Pare, core, and slice apples. Simmer in water until apples are tender: drain. Toss apples and cinnamon; set aside.
2. Combine sugar and flour. Cut in margarine and peanut butter. Combine one third of this mixture with the apples.
3. Spread a thin layer of the apple-peanut butter mixture on each crepe. Dot with remaining peanut butter mixture. Place on a baking sheet; do not fold.
4. Bake at 350°F 15 minutes. Cool 5 minutes; fold in half. Serve topped with ice cream, if desired.

4 filled crepes

Maple Apple Logs

2 cups pared, sliced baking apples*
¼ teaspoon cinnamon
⅓ cup raisins
⅓ cup walnuts, chopped
¼ cup maple syrup
2 tablespoons dark brown sugar
¼ cup water
12 dessert crepes
¾ cup Maple Nut Sauce (see page 90)

1. Simmer apples, cinnamon, raisins, nuts, maple syrup, and brown sugar in water until apples can be mashed and there is very little liquid left. Mash apples with a fork, leaving some chunky pieces.
2. Assemble, using jelly-roll method. Place rolls in a baking dish.
3. Bake at 375°F 15 minutes.
4. Serve 2 or 3 logs per serving topped with Maple Nut Sauce.

4 to 6 servings

*1½ cups apple butter may be substituted for apples, cinnamon, maple syrup, and dark brown sugar.

Apple Custard Tart

2 cooking apples
½ cup water
1 tablespoon butter or margarine
1 teaspoon maple syrup
1 tablespoon firmly packed brown sugar
¼ teaspoon pumpkin pie spice
½ cup walnuts, chopped
3 eggs, separated
¼ teaspoon cream of tartar
Dash salt
⅔ cup sugar
8 dessert crepes

1. Pare, core, and slice apples. Simmer apple slices in ½ cup water until tender but still firm. Set aside.
2. Melt butter. Stir in maple syrup, brown sugar, and pumpkin pie spice. Add apples and nuts; simmer 5 minutes. Remove from heat.
3. Beat egg whites with cream of tartar and salt. Gradually add sugar, beating until stiff and glossy. Fold apple mixture into egg whites.
4. Assemble, using tart method; use 2 to 3 tablespoons of fluffy apple mixture as filling.
5. Bake at 325°F 30 minutes. Cool for at least 1 hour. Remove from baking cups and serve.

8 tarts

Apricot-Nut Custard Foldovers

1 can (17 ounces) apricot halves
4 dessert crepes
1 cup Creamy Nut Sauce (see page 91)

Arrange 4 apricot halves down center of crepe. Fold sides over. Top with sauce. Garnish with a piece of apricot and serve.

4 filled crepes

Banana-Apricot Rolls

4 bananas, cut in half crosswise
5 tablespoons butter or margarine
8 dessert crepes
3 tablespoons light brown sugar
3 tablespoons apricot preserves
⅓ cup rum

1. Sauté bananas in 2 tablespoons butter in a skillet.
2. Place ½ banana in each crepe and fold, using egg-roll method.
3. Combine remaining butter, brown sugar, apricot preserves, and rum. Simmer, stirring constantly, until mixture is foamy and thick.
4. Coat banana rolls with hot syrup. Serve warm.

8 filled crepes

Banana-Nut Rolls

6 large bananas
¾ cup finely chopped nuts
12 dessert crepes
6 tablespoons butter
4 tablespoons sugar
¼ cup Grand Marnier

1. Bake bananas in skins at 350°F 20 minutes. Remove skins. Cut in half.
2. Sprinkle nuts over crepes. Place ½ banana in center of each crepe. Fold, using egg-roll method.
3. Melt butter and sugar in a skillet and cook to a clear brown syrup. Add Grand Marnier; stir until smooth. Place banana-nut rolls in syrup, turning to coat thoroughly. Serve immediately.

6 servings

Cannoli Cones

1 cup ricotta cheese
⅓ cup confectioners' sugar
¼ teaspoon cinnamon
1 teaspoon vanilla extract
¼ cup chopped maraschino cherries
¼ cup semisweet chocolate pieces
12 dessert crepes
   Chocolate curls or colored coconut

1. Beat ricotta cheese, sugar, cinnamon, and vanilla extract until fluffy. Add cherries and chocolate pieces. Chill 2 hours.
2. To assemble: spread a very thin layer of cheese mixture on entire crepe. Put a heaped tablespoon of mixture on ¼ of each crepe. Fold into a cone. Garnish and serve.

12 cones

Cheesecake Tarts

1 package (8 ounces) cream cheese
1 egg, slightly beaten
⅓ cup sugar
1½ teaspoons lemon juice
½ teaspoon vanilla extract
  Pinch cinnamon
4 dessert crepes
1 cup fresh fruit (blueberries,
  sliced strawberries, sliced
  peaches) or prepared pie filling

1. Beat cream cheese and egg. Blend in sugar, lemon juice, vanilla extract, and cinnamon.
2. Assemble, using tart method.
3. Bake at 350°F 25 minutes. Cool 15 minutes; remove from baking cups.
4. Top with fresh fruit or canned pie filling.

4 tarts

Cherries Jubilee

1 package (16 ounces) frozen
  pitted tart cherries
⅓ cup sugar
¾ cup Cherry Heering
  Dash salt
1 tablespoon cornstarch
1 tablespoon butter or
  margarine
1 tablespoon grated lemon peel
18 dessert crepes
¼ cup brandy
1 pint vanilla ice cream

1. Thaw cherries, drain, and reserve juice.
2. Combine juice (adding water to make 1 cup), sugar, ¼ cup Cherry Heering, salt, and cornstarch in chafing dish. Cook over medium heat, stirring constantly, until sauce begins to thicken. Stir in cherries, butter, and lemon peel. Simmer 3 minutes.
3. Using hot sauce method, fill chafing dish with crepes.
4. Warm ½ cup Cherry Heering and brandy in saucepan. Pour in chafing dish and ignite. When flames die down, place 3 crepes on a plate, top with vanilla ice cream, and spoon warm sauce and cherries over all.

6 servings

Quick Chocolate Mousse

1 package (4½ ounces) instant
  chocolate pudding and pie
  filling
1 cup cold milk
1 cup whipping cream, whipped
⅓ cup semisweet chocolate pieces
2 tablespoons crème de cacao
6 dessert crepes
  Whipped cream and grated
  chocolate for garnish (optional)

1. Combine pudding mix and milk. Stir until smooth. Fold into whipped cream. Chill 1 hour. Fold in chocolate pieces and crème de cacao.
2. Assemble, using tube method. Garnish, if desired.

6 servings

Choco-Mint Mousse: Substitute **4½ teaspoons crème de menthe** for crème de cacao.

Grand Marnier Chocolate Mousse: Substitute **2 tablespoons Grand Marnier** for crème de cacao.

Mocha Mousse: Add **2 tablespoons instant coffee** to whipped cream.

Black Forest: Spread each crepe with **1 tablespoon cherry preserves.** Top with chocolate mousse. Garnish with a **cherry.**

Chocolate-Nut Mousse: Add **⅓ cup chopped pecans, walnuts,** or **almonds** along with chocolate pieces.

Chocolate-Almond Torte

1 package (4½ ounces) chocolate.
    instant pudding and pie filling
2 cups milk
¼ teaspoon almond extract
12 dessert crepes
    Blanched almond halves

1. Prepare instant pudding and pie filling following package directions and using 2 cups milk; stir in almond extract.
2. Divide pudding on crepes and spread evenly. Stack the crepes and decorate top with almonds. Cut in wedges and serve.

6 servings

Coconut Roll

¼ cup butter or margarine
½ cup packed dark brown sugar
2 cups flaked coconut
2 tablespoons orange juice
¾ teaspoon grated orange peel
½ pint whipping cream
1 teaspoon sugar
½ teaspoon orange extract
8 dessert crepes

1. Melt butter. Stir in brown sugar, coconut, orange juice, and ½ teaspoon orange peel. Cook over medium heat until thick and caramel colored (about 3 to 4 minutes).
2. Whip cream with sugar until stiff. Fold in orange extract and ¼ teaspoon orange peel.
3. Assemble, using jelly-roll method; use coconut mixture as filling. Place on a baking sheet.
4. Bake at 375°F 5 minutes. Remove from baking sheet immediately. Serve 2 rolls per person, topped with whipped cream.

4 servings

Note: Filling can be stored in refrigerator for a week; orange flavor will become enhanced.

Coconut Macaroon Tortes

2 egg whites (at room
    temperature)
⅛ teaspoon cream of tartar
    Dash salt
¾ cup sifted granulated sugar
1 can (3½ ounces) flaked
    coconut
6 dessert crepes
1 pint ice cream or ½ pint
    whipping cream, whipped; or
    sliced fruit

1. Beat egg whites until foamy. Sprinkle in cream of tartar and salt. Continue beating until soft peaks form. Gradually sprinkle in sugar. Beat until stiff and glossy. Stir in coconut.
2. Spread a thin layer of coconut meringue on each crepe, leaving ⅛-inch border. Put on cookie sheets.
3. Bake at 325°F 20 minutes. Cool.
4. Torte is created by layering 3 macaroon crepes with ice cream, whipped cream, or fruit as filling.

2 tortes

Coconut-Peanut Stacks

¼ cup butter or margarine
¼ cup sugar
8 dessert crepes
1 cup peanuts
1 can (3½ ounces) flaked coconut
1 quart vanilla ice cream

1. Cream butter and sugar. Spread this mixture on crepes. Place crepes on a cookie sheet.
2. Chop nuts and coconut to medium-fine consistency. Set aside 4 tablespoons of the coconut-nut mixture to use for topping. Sprinkle remaining mixture over crepes.
3. Broil, watching closely, until just golden brown. Cool before removing from cookie sheet.
4. Divide half of the ice cream among four crepes. Top each with a coconut-nut crepe and remaining ice cream. Sprinkle each stack with remaining coconut-nut mixture.

8 servings

Cranberry Cream

1 can (16 ounces) whole
    cranberry sauce
1 package (3 ounces)
    orange-flavored gelatin
1 container (4½ ounces) frozen
    whipped topping, defrosted
8 dessert crepes

1. Heat half of the cranberry sauce. Stir in gelatin. Heat and stir until gelatin is dissolved. Cool 5 minutes. Stir in remaining cranberry sauce and whipped topping. Chill 1 hour.
2. Spread mixture on crepes and roll up jelly-roll fashion. Serve immediately.

8 filled crepes

Note: Filling refrigerates well for 1 week.

Crepes Suzette

½ cup butter
2 tablespoons shredded orange
    peel
3 tablespoons sugar
1 large orange, juiced
½ medium lemon, juiced
3 tablespoons curaçao
3 tablespoons Grand Marnier
18 dessert crepes
½ cup cognac

1. Cream butter, orange peel, and sugar. Put this mixture into the blazer of a chafing dish, or an electric frypan at 325°F. Melt, stirring constantly. Add fruit juices. Stir in curaçao and Grand Marnier. Continue cooking until sauce thickens and starts to bubble and boil.
2. Dip and fold crepes according to the hot sauce method.
3. When all crepes are coated, spread them evenly over the bottom of the blazer or frypan and continue cooking. Pour cognac over the top of the crepes, allow to warm, and ignite it. Serve when flame has gone out.

6 servings

Date-Nut Stacks

½ cup sugar
½ cup undiluted evaporated milk
2 egg yolks, slightly beaten
2 tablespoons butter or margarine
½ teaspoon vanilla extract
⅓ cup packed chopped dates
½ cup walnuts, chopped
½ cup flaked coconut
6 dessert crepes

1. Combine sugar, evaporated milk, egg yolks, and butter. Cook, stirring constantly, until thick and just to boiling point. Stir in vanilla extract, ¼ cup dates, nuts, and coconut. Cook 3 to 5 minutes. Mixture will be thick and caramel colored.
2. Spread mixture on crepes. Place on a baking sheet. Broil 2 to 3 minutes. (Watch closely; they burn very easily.) Remove from broiler.
3. To serve, stack 3 crepes on top of each other and garnish with remaining dates. Each stack serves 3 to 4 people.

6 to 8 servings

Lemon-Cheese Rolls

1 package (8 ounces) cream cheese
   (at room temperature)
1 can (14 ounces) sweetened
   condensed milk
5 tablespoons lemon juice
1 teaspoon grated lemon peel
½ teaspoon vanilla extract
10 dessert crepes
   Fresh fruit pieces

1. With an electric mixer, whip cream cheese. Slowly add condensed milk. Continue beating until free from lumps. Blend in lemon juice, peel, and vanilla extract. Chill 1½ to 2 hours.
2. To assemble, spread about ¼ cup mixture over crepe and roll up jelly-roll fashion. Serve topped with fruit. (This is a very sweet dessert, so the fruit does not need sugar.)

10 rolls

Note: If desired, assemble by spreading half the crepe with lemon-cheese mixture; fold in half and spread remaining mixture on top. Also, fresh fruit can be spooned on filling before folding.

Lemon Crepes

2 tablespoons butter or
   margarine
6 tablespoons sugar
1 teaspoon grated lemon peel
½ cup lemon juice
½ cup orange liqueur
18 dessert crepes
   Vanilla ice cream (optional)

1. Melt butter over medium heat. Add sugar; stir and cook until dissolved. Add lemon peel and juice and orange liqueur. Simmer about 5 minutes.
2. Add crepes, using hot sauce method. Delicious served warm with vanilla ice cream.

18 filled crepes

Lemon Meringue Stacks

1 can (16 ounces) lemon pie filling
9 Angel Crepes (see page 70)

1. Spread lemon pie filling ¼ inch thick on the back (the crepe side) of 6 Angel Crepes.
2. For each stack, place a plain Angel Crepe on the serving plate and top it with 2 of the Angel Crepes that have been spread with lemon filling.
3. To serve, cut each stack into 3 or 4 wedges.

9 to 12 servings

Mandarin Grape Salad

½ teaspoon minced crystallized
   ginger
8 ounces plain yogurt
1 can (11 ounces) mandarin
   oranges, drained
1 cup green grape halves
6 dessert crepes
6 orange sections and 6 grape
   halves for garnish

1. Combine ginger and yogurt. Toss orange sections and grape halves with half of the yogurt mixture.
2. Assemble, using tube method, on individual serving plates. Top with remaining yogurt mixture and garnish with a mandarin orange section and grape half.

6 filled crepes

Sweet Manicotti

16 ounces creamed cottage cheese,
    drained
 1 tablespoon sugar
 ½ teaspoon grated lemon peel
 1 egg, slightly beaten
 3 tablespoons macaroon crumbs
12 dessert crepes
 2 cups Fruit Sauce (see page 91)

1. Combine drained cottage cheese, sugar, lemon peel, and egg. Beat until smooth and creamy. Stir in macaroon crumbs.
2. Assemble, using tube method. Snugly fit into baking dish. Cover with plastic film and refrigerate 1 hour.
3. Bake uncovered at 350°F 20 minutes. Cool 5 minutes.
4. Top with Fruit Sauce. Serve two rolls for dessert, three for breakfast.

12 filled crepes

Mincemeat Logs with Hard Sauce

 1 can (16 ounces) mincemeat pie
    filling
12 dessert crepes
 1 cup warm Rum Hard Sauce (see
    page 91)

1. Heat mincemeat until bubbling.
2. Assemble, using tube method, on individual serving plates. Serve immediately topped with warm hard sauce.

12 logs

Mincemeat Rolls

 1 can (16 ounces) mincemeat pie
    filling
 ½ cup chopped walnuts or pecans
12 warm dessert crepes
 1 quart vanilla ice cream

1. Combine mincemeat and nuts.
2. Spread 2½ to 3 tablespoons of this mixture on each warm crepe. Roll up, jelly-roll fashion.
3. Serve topped with ice cream.

12 rolls

Mincemeat Squares with Lemon Sauce

 1 can (16 ounces) mincemeat pie
    filling
12 dessert crepes
 1 cup Sweet Lemon Sauce (see page
    90)

1. With mincemeat as filling, assemble using square turnover method. Place on a baking sheet.
2. Bake at 375°F 10 minutes. Serve warm with lemon sauce.

12 squares

Peaches 'n' Cream

½ pint whipping cream
1 teaspoon vanilla extract
2 tablespoons sugar
1 cup fresh peaches, peeled and
    sliced (see Note)
8 dessert crepes
¼ cup confectioners' sugar

1. Whip cream; add vanilla extract and sugar. Fold in fresh fruit.
2. Assemble, using tube method. Sprinkle with confectioners' sugar.

8 filled crepes

Note: If desired, substitute for peaches 1 cup strawberries, hulled and sliced, 1 cup whole raspberries, 1 cup whole blueberries, or ½ cup sliced peaches and ½ cup whole raspberries.

Peach Melba

2 packages (10 ounces each) frozen
    raspberries
2 tablespoons cornstarch
⅓ cup currant jelly
¼ cup orange marmalade
6 medium peaches, peeled and
    sliced
18 dessert crepes
½ cup Italian brandy

1. Drain and reserve berries. Measure syrup; add water to equal 2 cups.
2. In blazer of chafing dish or electric frypan, combine liquid and cornstarch; bring to boiling, stirring constantly. Boil 5 minutes. Stir in jelly, marmalade, peaches, and berries. Simmer 5 minutes.
3. Assemble, using hot sauce method. Flame by pouring warmed brandy over folded coated crepes and fruit, and ignite.
4. Serve crepes when flames go out. Top with fruit and sauce.

6 servings

Pears with Almond Sauce

6 fresh medium pears
2 tablespoons lemon juice
¼ teaspoon vanilla extract
1 cup sugar
    Water
    Dash salt
1½ tablespoons cornstarch
1 cup light cream or half-and-half
1 egg yolk, slightly beaten
1 tablespoon Amaretto
1 tablespoon chopped almonds
8 dessert crepes

1. Pare, core, and slice pears into eighths or twelfths.
2. In a saucepan toss pears with lemon juice, vanilla extract, and ¾ cup sugar. Add enough water to just cover fruit. Simmer 25 to 30 minutes, or until pears are tender. Cool.
3. Make a sauce by combining ¼ cup sugar, salt, and cornstarch. Gradually add cream, stirring constantly. Beat in egg yolk. Cook over medium heat, stirring constantly, until mixture comes to boiling. Remove from heat immediately. Stir in Amaretto and almonds.
4. To assemble, place sliced pears on half of crepe, fold unfilled half over pears, and top with sauce.

8 filled crepes

Pears in Chocolate Nests

2 cups sliced cooked pears
6 Chocolate Angel Crepes (see
    page 71)
    Grated semisweet chocolate

Arrange pear slices on top of each crepe. Garnish with grated chocolate and serve.

6 servings

Note: If desired, stack the crepes and fruit: crepe, fruit, crepe, fruit. Garnish with grated chocolate. Cut into 2 or 3 wedges per stack.

Mocha Pecan Stacks

¼ **cup sugar**
1 **tablespoon instant coffee**
 Dash salt
1 **cup whipping cream**
½ **cup chopped pecans**
12 **cocoa crepes (see page 11)**
 Unsweetened chocolate, shaved or grated

1. Combine sugar, coffee, salt, and cream. Stir until well blended. Chill 30 minutes.
2. Whip cream until stiff. Fold in pecans.
3. Spread mixture over crepes. Make three stacks of 4 crepes each or stack as desired. Top with chocolate.
4. To serve, cut into wedges.

6 to 9 servings

Pears and Fudge

2 **cups sliced cooked pears**
6 **dessert crepes**
¾ **cup fudge sauce (bottled or see page 89)**
⅓ **cup chopped pecans**

1. Warm pears. Drain.
2. Assemble, using tube method, on individual serving plates. Top with 2 tablespoons fudge sauce and 1 tablespoon chopped nuts.

6 servings

Pineapple-Coconut Stacks

2 **tablespoons butter or margarine**
¼ **cup brown sugar**
1 **cup flaked coconut**
8 **dessert crepes**
1 **cup pineapple pie filling**

1. Melt butter. Stir in brown sugar and coconut. Cook over medium heat until well blended, thick, and caramel colored.
2. Spread mixture on 4 crepes. Place on a baking sheet.
3. Spread remaining 4 crepes with pineapple filling (these will not be broiled).
4. Broil coconut crepes 3 to 5 minutes. Watch these closely, they burn easily.
5. To assemble the stack, first put a pineapple crepe on a serving plate, next a hot coconut crepe, then another pineapple crepe, and top with a hot coconut crepe.
6. Serve by cutting each stack into 3 or 4 wedges.

6 to 8 servings

Pineapple-Strawberry Crepes

1 **large fresh pineapple**
1½ **cups Strawberry Sauce (see page 91)**
8 **dessert crepes**

1. Pare, core, and cut pineapple into spears, ½ inch thick and up to 6 inches long. Toss pineapple with ½ cup Strawberry Sauce. Chill 1 hour.
2. Spoon pineapple into crepes, using tube method. Serve topped with remaining sauce.

8 filled crepes

Pumpkin Fluff

1 can (16 ounces) pumpkin pie filling
1 container (4½ ounces) frozen whipped topping, defrosted
1 cup Caramel Sauce (see page 90)
⅓ cup raisins
12 dessert crepes

1. Combine pumpkin filling and whipped topping. Spread a thin layer (⅛ to ¼ inch) on each crepe. Roll up jelly-roll fashion.
2. Place on individual serving plates. Top with sauce and sprinkle with raisins.

12 filled crepes

Gingersnap Pumpkin Fluff: Follow recipe for Pumpkin Fluff; sprinkle **1 cup crushed gingersnaps** over the pumpkin filling before rolling up. Top with **whipped cream** and some **gingersnap crumbs.**

Maple Nut Pumpkin Fluff: Follow recipe for Pumpkin Fluff; use **Maple Nut Sauce** (see page 90) as a topping instead of Caramel Sauce.

Prune Rolls with Custard Sauce

12 ounces pitted dried prunes, quartered
½ cup water
1½ teaspoons brandy flavoring
¼ teaspoon grated lemon peel
6 dessert crepes
½ cup Custard Sauce (see page 90)

1. Simmer quartered prunes in water until most of the water is absorbed and prunes fall apart easily. Mash prunes. Stir in brandy flavoring and lemon peel. Cook 2 minutes, stirring constantly.
2. Spread about 2 tablespoons of prune mixture on each crepe and roll up jelly-roll fashion. Serve topped with Custard Sauce.

6 rolls

Hot Prune Squares

12 ounces pitted dried prunes
½ cup water
2 teaspoons brandy flavoring
3 tablespoons orange marmalade
6 dessert crepes

1. Simmer prunes in water until most of water is absorbed and prunes break apart easily. Mash prunes. Stir in brandy flavoring and 2 tablespoons marmalade.
2. Assemble, using square turnover method. Place, seam side down, on a baking sheet.
3. Bake at 375°F 10 minutes. Brush with remaining marmalade and serve warm.

6 squares

Chocolate-Almond Torte (bottom), 74;
Mocha Pecan Stacks (top), 79

Rhubarb-Topped Ice Cream Logs

2½ cups diced rhubarb
½ cup water
Dash salt
½ cup white sugar
½ cup brown sugar
1½ tablespoons tapioca
1 quart vanilla ice cream (or strawberry)
12 dessert crepes

1. Combine rhubarb, water, and salt in a saucepan. Cover and simmer over medium heat, 10 to 15 minutes. Fruit should be very tender and cooked down similar to the consistency of applesauce. Stir in sugars. Continue cooking until sugar is dissolved. Add tapioca. Remove from heat and let stand 5 minutes. Return to heat; simmer 3 minutes. Cover and let stand off the heat until it thickens and is cool.
2. To assemble, cut ice cream into spears or sticks. Roll up in crepes, using tube method. Top with sauce and serve.

12 logs

Note: The sauce refrigerates well for 5 days.

Strawberry Rhubarb-Topped Ice Cream Logs: Follow recipe for Rhubarb-Topped Ice Cream Logs; add **1 cup sliced fresh strawberries** to rhubarb before cooking.

Strawberry Short Crepe

1 pint fresh strawberries
½ pint whipping cream
2 teaspoons sugar
¼ teaspoon vanilla extract
6 Angel Crepes (see page 70)
Whole strawberries for garnish (optional)

1. Wash, hull, and slice berries; reserve.
2. Whip cream; beat in sugar and vanilla extract.
3. To assemble, spoon berries on top of 4 Angel Crepes. Stack one berried crepe on top of another berried crepe, making 2 stacks of 2. Top with a plain Angel Crepe and whipped cream. If desired, garnish with a whole berry. Cut each stack into 3 or 4 wedges.

6 to 8 servings

Note: Blueberries, raspberries, peaches, or apricots can be substituted for strawberries.

Strawberries in Banana Cream

2 pints strawberries
Sugar
2 tablespoons water
¼ cup sugar
1 egg yolk, slightly beaten
4 large ripe bananas, mashed
½ cup whipping cream, whipped
12 dessert crepes

1. Wash and hull strawberries. Add sugar to taste. Let stand at least 30 minutes.
2. Bring water and sugar to boiling in top of a double boiler. Remove from heat. Cool to room temperature.
3. Stir egg yolk into cooled syrup. Cook over boiling water until creamy and thick. Cool to room temperature. Fold in bananas and whipped cream.
4. Place strawberries in crepes, following the tube method.
5. To serve, place the filled crepe on a dessert plate and top with approximately ¼ cup banana cream.

12 filled crepes

Cherries Jubilee, 73

Tortoni Logs

⅔ cup crushed macaroons
12 maraschino cherries, quartered
1 teaspoon brandy flavoring
⅓ cup chopped toasted almonds
1 quart vanilla ice cream, softened
8 dessert crepes
1 cup whipped cream
8 whole almonds

1. Combine macaroons, cherries, brandy flavoring, chopped nuts, and ice cream. Freeze until firm (about 2 hours).
2. Slice ice cream mixture into 8 spears. Roll each spear in a crepe. Serve immediately, topped with whipped cream and almonds.

8 logs

Spumoni Logs: Follow recipe for Tortoni Logs; substitute **Pistachio Sauce** (page 91) for whipped cream and almonds.

Crepes with Walnuts (Palatschinken)

Palatschinken is what the Yugoslavians call their traditional walnut and sugar crepes.

¼ cup butter or margarine
¼ cup sugar
¼ teaspoon vanilla extract
1 cup grated walnuts
8 dessert crepes

1. Cream butter, sugar, and vanilla extract. Spread butter-sugar mixture on hot (not warm) crepes and sprinkle with walnuts.
2. Assemble, using jelly-roll method. Serve on a heated platter.

Note: If desired, vary recipe by adding ¼ cup semisweet chocolate pieces with nuts, serving with hot fudge sauce on top, or adding ¼ teaspoon cinnamon to sugar mixture and topping log with whipped cream.

Hot Curried Fruit Squares

⅓ cup unsweetened applesauce*
3 tablespoons brown sugar
1 tablespoon butter or margarine
1 tablespoon chunky peanut butter
½ teaspoon curry powder
2 cups assorted fresh fruit slices
  (pears, peaches, apricots,
  cherries, pineapple, banana); or
  two 8-ounce cans fruits for
  salad or tropical fruit salad
4 dessert crepes
  Flaked coconut (optional)

1. Make a sweet curry sauce by heating the applesauce and adding the brown sugar, butter, chunky peanut butter, and curry powder. Blend thoroughly. Remove from heat.
2. Remove 1 tablespoon of sauce. Fold the fruit into the remaining sauce.
3. Assemble, using square turnover method. Brush reserved sauce over the tops of the fruit squares.
4. Bake at 350°F 10 minutes. Serve warm garnished with flaked coconut, if desired.

4 servings

Note: The filling may be refrigerated.

*If sweetened applesauce is used, decrease sugar to 2 tablespoons.

SAUCES

Basic White Sauce

¼ cup butter or margarine
5 tablespoons flour
2 cups milk
¼ teaspoon salt

1. Melt butter over low heat. Stir in flour. Gradually add milk, stirring constantly. Cook and stir until mixture comes to boiling; boil 1 minute.
2. Remove from heat. Mix in salt.

2 cups sauce

Dijon Sauce: Follow recipe for Basic White Sauce; blend in **2 tablespoons Dijon mustard** after adding milk.

Curry Sauce: Follow recipe for Basic White Sauce; blend **2 teaspoons curry powder** and **⅛ teaspoon dry mustard** into sauce after adding milk.

Parmesan Sauce: Follow recipe for Basic White Sauce; after sauce has thickened, stir in **⅓ cup grated Parmesan cheese.** Remove from heat.

Standard Hollandaise

¼ pound butter or margarine
3 egg yolks
2 tablespoons lemon juice
  Pinch salt
  Dash nutmeg
  Dash cayenne pepper
2 tablespoons hot water

1. Melt butter (do not brown) and keep hot.
2. Put egg yolks in top of double boiler over hot (not boiling) water. Beat until smooth but not fluffy. Add lemon juice and dry seasonings; drizzle in butter and hot water. Beat with a whisk until sauce begins to thicken. Do not reheat.

1 cup sauce

Béarnaise Sauce: Combine **¼ cup dry white wine, 2 scallions, chopped, ½ teaspoon dried tarragon, pinch fresh ground pepper,** and **¼ cup vinegar.** Simmer over medium heat until reduced to 2 tablespoons. Follow recipe for Standard Hollandaise. Blend in liquid along with butter.

Dilled Cucumber Hollandaise: Follow recipe for Standard Hollandaise; add **½ cup chopped cucumber** and **½ teaspoon dried dill weed** to mixture immediately after butter has been added.

Hollandaise Verde: Follow recipe for Standard Hollandaise; chop **3 sprigs parsley, 1 whole scallion,** and **1 tablespoon capers.** Combine with **2 teaspoons Worcestershire sauce** and add to mixture immediately after butter has been added.

Blender Hollandaise

½ cup butter or margarine
3 egg yolks*
1½ tablespoons lemon juice
⅛ teaspoon salt
 Dash cayenne pepper

1. Heat butter until just bubbling (do not brown).
2. Put egg yolks, lemon juice, salt, and cayenne into an electric blender. Turn blender on then off (medium speed) just to blend. Turn on blender (medium speed) and pour melted butter in a steady stream into egg yolk mixture. Turn off blender as soon as all the butter is added.
3. Serve at once while warm. (Sauce can be kept warm over hot but not boiling water.)

⅔ cup sauce

*Use egg whites in a meringue dessert.

Curried Cheese Sauce

¼ cup butter or margarine
5 tablespoons flour
1½ teaspoons curry powder
1½ cups milk
¼ pound extra sharp Cheddar cheese, coarsely grated
¼ teaspoon Worcestershire sauce
 Dash cayenne pepper

1. Melt butter over low heat. Add flour. Cook and stir 1 minute. Add curry powder.
2. Gradually add milk, stirring constantly. Cook over medium heat, stirring continuously until smooth and thickened.
3. Stir in cheese, Worcestershire sauce, and cayenne. Continue stirring until cheese melts.

2 cups sauce

Note: Sauce freezes well.

Rich Cheese Sauce

¼ cup butter or margarine
5 tablespoons flour
1½ cups milk
¼ teaspoon Worcestershire sauce
¼ teaspoon salt
¼ pound extra sharp Cheddar cheese, coarsely shredded

1. Melt butter over low heat. Stir in flour. Cook 1 minute.
2. Gradually add milk and Worcestershire sauce, stirring constantly. Cook and stir until mixture begins to boil. Remove from heat.
3. Add salt. Stir in cheese until melted.

2 cups sauce

Cheddar Cheese Sauce

2 tablespoons butter or margarine
1 tablespoon flour
½ teaspoon paprika
1¼ teaspoon dry mustard
¼ teaspoon salt
 Few grains cayenne pepper
2 cups milk
4 ounces sharp Cheddar cheese, finely shredded

1. Melt the butter in a saucepan. Blend the flour, paprika, dry mustard, salt, and cayenne pepper into the butter. Heat until bubbly. Add the milk gradually, stirring constantly. Cook 1 to 2 minutes.
2. Remove from the heat. Add the cheese and stir until blended and sauce is smooth.

About 2 cups sauce

Creamy Curry Sauce

- 2 tablespoons butter or margarine
- 3 tablespoons finely chopped onion
- 2 tablespoons flour
- 3 tablespoons chunky peanut butter
- 1¼ cups unsweetened applesauce
- 2 to 3 teaspoons Curry Powder (see page 40)
- ½ cup chicken stock
  Salt

Melt butter. Sauté onion until soft. Stir in flour, peanut butter, applesauce, Curry Powder, and stock. Simmer, stirring constantly, for 5 minutes. Season with salt to taste.

About 1½ cups sauce

Note: This sauce stores well in the refrigerator for 1 week.

Barbecue Sauce

- ½ cup finely chopped onion
- 2 tablespoons oil
- ½ cup ketchup
- 1 tablespoon Worcestershire sauce
- 2 tablespoons dark brown sugar
- 2 tablespoons dry mustard
- ¼ cup vinegar
- ¼ teaspoon pepper
- ½ teaspoon Tabasco

1. Sauté onion in oil. Add remaining ingredients.
2. Simmer 15 to 20 minutes.

2 cups sauce

Spanish Sauce

- 1 can (16 ounces) tomatoes
- 1 medium onion
- 2 stalks celery
- 1 medium green pepper
- 1 small clove garlic, crushed in a garlic press
- 1 tablespoon vegetable oil
- ¼ teaspoon salt
- ⅛ teaspoon pepper

1. Drain tomatoes; reserve juice. Coarsely chop tomatoes, onion, celery, and green pepper. Combine with garlic and sauté in oil until vegetables are tender.
2. Add reserved tomato juice, salt, and pepper. Simmer until most of the liquid is absorbed, but sauce is still moist.

1½ cups sauce

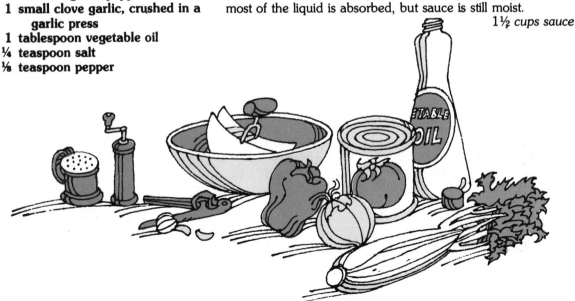

Quick Marinara Sauce

¼ cup chopped onion
1 tablespoon oil
1 can (16 ounces) stewed
    tomatoes
1 clove garlic, crushed in a
    garlic press
½ teaspoon oregano
    Pinch rosemary
    Pinch basil
4 fennel seeds, crushed
    Dash cayenne pepper
    Salt

1. Sauté onion in hot oil until clear. Add tomatoes, breaking up any large pieces of tomato. Stir in dry seasonings, except salt.
2. Simmer, uncovered, to reduce liquid, about 20 minutes. Salt to taste.

About 1½ cups sauce

Thick Marinara Sauce: Add **2 teaspoons cornstarch** when cooking tomato mixture.

Smooth Marinara Sauce: Follow recipe for Quick Marinara Sauce; place tomatoes in electric blender container and blend until smooth before adding to sautéed onion.

Quick Creamy Fish Sauce

1 can (about 10 ounces)
    condensed cream of mushroom
    or cream of celery soup
2 whole scallions, chopped
½ teaspoon thyme leaves

1. Combine all ingredients; simmer until scallions are tender.
2. Serve with tuna, flounder, cod, or sole.

About 1 cup sauce

Chili Sauce

1 can (28 ounces) tomatoes, diced
2 teaspoons arrowroot or 1 teaspoon
    cornstarch
1 large onion, chopped
1 medium green pepper, diced
1 large clove garlic, crushed in
    a garlic press
2 tablespoons vegetable oil
1 tablespoon chili powder
½ teaspoon salt
¼ teaspoon sugar

1. Put tomatoes with juice in saucepan. Stir in arrowroot. Mix in onion, green pepper, garlic, oil, chili powder, salt, and sugar.
2. Simmer, covered, 15 minutes. Remove cover, and continue to simmer until liquid is reduced by about half.

About 2 cups sauce

John's Orange Sauce

1 can (6 ounces) frozen orange
    juice
¼ cup jellied cranberry sauce
¼ cup currant jelly
¾ cup orange marmalade
1 tablespoon orange peel
1 tablespoon lemon peel
1 tablespoon maraschino cherry
    juice
1 cup water
3 tablespoons cornstarch
3 tablespoons Grand Marnier

1. In a saucepan, combine orange juice, cranberry sauce, currant jelly, marmalade, orange peel, lemon peel, cherry juice, and ¾ cup water. Bring to boiling. Remove from heat.
2. Combine cornstarch with ¼ cup water; stir into hot fruit sauce. Bring to boiling, stirring constantly. Stir in Grand Marnier, bring to boiling, and remove from heat.

About 3 cups sauce

Pesto Sauce

This spicy nut-and-cheese sauce is excellent with vegetables, eggs, fish, or poultry.

1½ to 2 teaspoons dried basil
  3 tablespoons chopped walnuts
  3 tablespoons grated Parmesan
    cheese
  1 medium clove garlic, crushed in
    a garlic press
  3 sprigs fresh parsley
  1 tablespoon olive oil
  2 tablespoons vegetable oil
  2 tablespoons butter or
    margarine, melted

1. In an electric blender, combine basil, nuts, cheese, garlic, and parsley. Blend at medium speed until nuts are the size of a split pea.
2. Combine oils and butter. Slowly pour this liquid into blender while it is still on medium speed. Turn off as soon as liquid is added. It's ready to serve.

About ⅓ cup sauce

Lemon Sauce

  2 tablespoons butter or
    margarine
2½ tablespoons flour
  ½ cup whipping cream
  ½ cup water
  ¼ teaspoon salt
  1 tablespoon lemon juice

1. Melt butter over low heat. Stir in flour; blend well.
2. Add cream and water gradually, stirring constantly. Over medium heat, stir and bring to boiling. Boil 1 minute. Add salt and lemon juice. Remove from heat.

1 cup sauce

Mushroom Sauce

  ½ pound mushrooms, cleaned and
    coarsely chopped
  3 cups water
  3 beef bouillon cubes
  ⅓ cup butter
  ⅓ cup flour

1. Simmer mushrooms, water, and bouillon cubes, uncovered, 20 minutes.
2. Melt butter. Stir in flour. Cook 2 minutes over medium heat, stirring constantly. Add mushrooms and broth; mix well. Bring to boiling. Boil 1 minute.

2 cups sauce

Rich Sauce for Fish

3 tablespoons butter or
    margarine, melted
3 tablespoons flour
1 cup light cream or half-and-half
2 egg yolks, slightly beaten
2 tablespoons lemon juice
¼ teaspoon thyme
⅛ teaspoon salt
    Dash pepper

1. Make a roux with 2 tablespoons of butter and flour. Slowly stir in cream. Cook until thick. Stir a little of the hot sauce into egg yolks. Slowly stir this egg yolk mixture into the rest of the sauce. Mix in lemon juice and thyme; season with salt and pepper. If necessary, keep warm over hot water.
2. Serve with fish.

About 1 cup sauce

Peach Chutney

1 cup peach preserves
½ cup golden raisins
¼ cup chopped pecans or walnuts
¼ cup cider vinegar
½ teaspoon orange peel
1 tablespoon chopped crystallized
    ginger
1 teaspoon instant minced onion

1. In a saucepan, combine all ingredients. Cook 3 to 5 minutes.
2. Cool 1 hour before serving. Store in refrigerator.

1½ cups chutney

Creamy Lemon Sauce

¼ cup whipping cream
3 ounces cream cheese, softened
2 tablespoons lemon juice
2 tablespoons butter or margarine,
    melted
    Dash salt
    Dash cayenne pepper

1. Whip cream. Gradually add small pieces of softened cream cheese. Blend in lemon juice, butter, salt, and cayenne.
2. Serve with vegetables and fish.

1 cup sauce

Creamy Brown Sauce: Follow recipe for Creamy Lemon Sauce; substitute a **beef bouillon cube** dissolved in **2 tablespoons hot water** for lemon juice. Taste before adding salt.

Fudge Sauce

3 ounces (3 squares) unsweetened
    chocolate
¼ cup butter
⅔ cup sugar
⅛ teaspoon salt
⅔ undiluted evaporated milk
1 teaspoon vanilla extract
    Few drops almond extract

1. Melt chocolate and butter in the top of a double boiler over boiling water. Remove from teat and stir in sugar and salt. Gradually add evaporated milk, blending well.
2. Cook over boiling water, stirring constantly, about 4 minutes. Remove from heat and stir in vanilla and almond extracts. Serve warm.

About 1½ cups sauce

Apple Sauce

1 can (12 ounces) apple juice
2 tablespoons brown sugar
1 tablespoon cornstarch
¼ teaspoon ground cinnamon
2 tablespoons lemon juice
1 tablespoon butter

1. Pour apple juice into a saucepan and heat until hot.
2. Mix brown sugar, cornstarch, cinnamon, and lemon juice. Stir into hot apple juice. Bring to boiling, stirring constantly. Simmer about 10 minutes, or until slightly thickened.
3. Remove from heat and stir in butter. Serve warm on egg-and-sausage-filled crepes.

About 1¼ cups sauce

Maple Nut Sauce

½ cup dark corn syrup
⅓ cup chopped nuts
½ teaspoon maple flavoring
1 tablespoon melted butter

1. Stir all ingredients together until blended. Do not cook. Sauce is ready to serve.
2. Store in tightly covered jar at room temperature.

¾ cup sauce

Sweet Lemon Sauce

1 tablespoon butter or margarine
⅓ cup lemon juice
1½ teaspoons grated lemon peel
2 tablespoons cornstarch
⅛ teaspoon salt
¾ cup sugar
1 cup boiling water

1. Melt butter in a saucepan. Remove from heat; stir in lemon juice, lemon peel, and a mixture of cornstarch, salt, and sugar. Stir until well blended.
2. Gradually add boiling water, stirring constantly. Return to heat; boil gently 5 minutes. Serve warm or cooled.

About 1½ cups sauce

Custard Sauce

1 package (3¾ ounces) vanilla instant pudding and pie filling
2 cups cold milk
¼ cup fresh orange juice

Prepare pudding mix with 2 cups milk as directed on package. Stir in orange juice.

About 2¼ cups sauce

Note: May be stored, covered, in refrigerator for 1 day.

Almond Sauce: Follow recipe for Custard Sauce. Substitute **3 tablespoons almond liqueur** for the orange juice.

Caramel Sauce

1 cup light brown sugar
3 tablespoons water
1 tablespoon butter or margarine
1 tablespoon cornstarch
1 cup hot water
1 teaspoon vanilla extract

1. Cook sugar and 3 tablespoons water until the color of butterscotch. Remove from heat. Stir in butter and cornstarch until blended.
2. Add 1 cup hot water; cook over low heat until thickened. Stir in vanilla extract.

About 1½ cups sauce

Caramel Nut Sauce: *Add ⅓ cup chopped pecans or walnuts to Caramel Sauce.*

Strawberry Sauce

1 package (10 ounces) frozen
   strawberries
1 tablespoon cornstarch
¼ cup currant jell

1. Drain syrup from strawberries into a saucepan. Stir cornstarch into strawberry syrup. Cook cornstarch mixture until thickened, stirring constantly.

in berries and jelly; bring to boiling and remove from

1½ cups sauce

tores well in refrigerator 4 to 5 days.

Sauce: Follow recipe for Strawberry Sauce; substitute
ces **any frozen fruit** for strawberries.

Creamy

½ cup chopped
⅛ teaspoon map
1 cup Custard S

ts and maple flavoring into Custard Sauce.

1⅓ cups sauce

Finely chopped nut brittle may be substituted for nuts and
flavoring.

Pistachio

1 package (3¾
   instant pu
2¼ cups milk

re pudding mix as directed on package, using 2¼ cups

2¼ cups sauce

Rum Ha

⅓ cup butter
1½ cups confec
2 tablespoons

ream butter. Add sugar gradually, beating until fluffy. Add
extract; beat until well blended.
lay be used immediately or stored in refrigerator.

1½ cups sauce

FILLINGS FROM LEFTOVERS

Beef

- 2 cups diced cooked beef
- 1 cup Mushroom Sauce (see page 88)
  Dash Worcestershire sauce
- ⅓ cup sautéed onion

Smoked Ham

- 2 cups diced ham
- 1 cup Rich Cheese Sauce (see page 85)
- ¼ teaspoon dry mustard
- 1 can (8 ounces) peas and carrots, drained

Pork

- 2 cups diced cooked pork
- ¾ cup Basic White Sauce (see page 84)
- 3 tablespoons chili sauce
- ¼ cup shredded Cheddar cheese

Lamb

- 2 cups diced cooked lamb
- ¼ cup sautéed onion
- 1 cup Curried Cheese Sauce (see page 85)
- 2 tablespoons Peach Chutney (see page 89)

Veal

- 2 cups diced cooked veal
- ¼ cup sautéed onion
- ¼ cup sautéed green pepper
- ¾ cup Thick Marinara Sauce (see page 87)

Fish

- 2 cups cooked flaked fish
- ½ cup tartar sauce
- 1 cup Lemon Sauce (see page 88)
  Salt and pepper

Chicken

- 2 cups diced cooked chicken
- 1 cup Parmesan Sauce (see page 84)
- ¼ teaspoon poultry seasoning
- ½ cup chopped broccoli

Turkey

- 2 cups diced cooked turkey
- 2 slices crisp-fried bacon, crumbled
- 2 tablespoons raisins
- ¾ cup Creamy Curry Sauce (see page 86)

Duck

- 2 cups diced cooked duck
- ¾ cup John's Orange Sauce (see page 87)

For 8 dinner crepes: Combine all ingredients. Assemble, using a slotted spoon, turnover or tube method. Arrange in a baking pan. Spoon remaining sauce on top. Bake at 375°F 15 minutes.

INDEX